TALKING OF JUSTICE

Also by Leila Seth

We, the Children of India: The Preamble to Our Constitution (2010)
On Balance: An Autobiography (2003)

TALKING OF JUSTICE

j

PEOPLE'S RIGHTS
IN MODERN INDIA

LEILA SETH

ALEPH

ALEPH

ALEPH BOOK COMPANY
An independent publishing firm
promoted by *Rupa Publications India*

Published in India in 2014 by
Aleph Book Company
7/16 Ansari Road, Daryaganj
New Delhi 110 002

The author has asserted her moral rights.
Copyright © Leila Seth 2014

All rights reserved.

No part of this publication may be reproduced, transmitted, or stored in a retrieval system, in any form or by any means, without permission in writing from Aleph Book Company.

ISBN: 978-93-82277-96-5

1 3 5 7 9 10 8 6 4 2

Printed and bound in India by Replika Press Pvt. Ltd.

This book is sold subject to the condition that it shall not, by way of trade or otherwise, be lent, resold, hired out, or otherwise circulated without the publisher's prior consent in any form of binding or cover other than that in which it is published.

*To Vikram, Shantum, Aradhana and Gitu,
who teach me to be just*

One man's word is no man's word; we should quietly hear both sides.
                                   ~Goethe

Every reform was once private opinion...
                                   ~Emerson

Contents

Author's Note	xi
Rape: Inside the Justice Verma Committee	1
Gender Sensitization of the Judiciary	20
Social Action Litigation	37
Women's Rights	59
A Uniform Civil Code towards Gender Justice	71
Children's Rights	88
The Girl Child	108
Widows' Rights	126
Prisoners' Rights	137
Judicial Administration	160
You're Criminal if Gay	191
Acknowledgements	197
Chapter Notes	199
References	205

Author's Note

When David Davidar of Aleph Book Company asked me to write a short article about my experience as a member of the Justice J. S. Verma Committee (a three-person committee set up in the aftermath of the rape and murder of a young woman in Delhi in 2012), I was intrigued but not quite convinced. 'What will you do with a short article?' I asked him. He told me that he saw it as the opening chapter of a book drawn from selected lectures and speeches I had given over the course of my career. (See Chapter Notes on Page 199.) The idea appealed to me. The material has, however, been rewritten for this book.

After some discussion, we settled on the title *Talking of Justice*. This set me thinking: what, at root, is justice? When I speak to children about the Preamble to our Constitution, I explain justice as 'being fair'. But how can one be fair if the laws are not adequate and the interpreters of the law not sensitive? We need to change the laws and sensitize the judiciary. But that is not enough. The laws, judgments and decisions need to be implemented. This can only happen when society changes and accepts new ideas; and for this we need awareness and advocacy, assertion and adoption. A change in law can be brought about by a forward-thinking government; or by popular demand; or through social action litigation. The change in mindset, though, is a slower and more difficult process; and for this to take place education and openness are essential.

In order to see that justice is done, it is necessary to achieve a sense of equality either by creating it or by 'not treating unequals as equal'—I have examined this concept at greater length in the essay 'Gender Sensitization of the Judiciary'. Over the years, women have been treated as second-class citizens despite constituting half the human race. They are particularly vulnerable because of the patriarchal mindset that affects every aspect of their lives, including the birth, upbringing and marriage of the girl child.

Several of the essays in this book deal with some aspects of discrimination against the girl child and against women. However, as liberty and fraternity are also aspirations in our Preamble, I have dealt with the rights of children, especially the link between education and child labour, and the rights of prisoners and the effectiveness of prisons.

I have also included an essay on the subject of the Uniform Civil Code. This has become a contentious issue, but it is a Directive Principle of our Constitution and I am in favour of it. I sincerely believe that if it is properly formulated and implemented it will bring justice to all women in India.

We are all aware of the adage, 'Justice delayed is justice

Author's Note

denied.' Delays are at the root of many of the ills of the judicial system in India; this is addressed in the essay 'Judicial Administration'.

Lastly, it is important to appreciate the human element in delivering justice. A constitution is only as good as the people who interpret and implement it. The mindset of those passing judgments is a crucial element of this process, as can be seen in the case of Section 377 of the Indian Penal Code (dealing with the subject of homosexuality). On this issue, two judges of the Delhi High Court decided one way but were overruled four years later by two judges of the Supreme Court. However, in April 2014, in the transgender identity case, two judges of the Supreme Court showed a completely different mindset to that of the judges of the Supreme Court who decided the LGBT case. This certainly leads one to the belief that such cases should be decided by at least five judges.

Though most of the book deals with the girl child and women's rights, I have usually used the grammatical locutions 'he' and 'his' instead of 'he or she', 'his or hers' or 's/he'. This is to avoid cumbrous expressions, especially as the law clearly provides that 'he' includes 'she'. Needless to say, this is not to accept that he is better than she. However, although many refer to this century as 'the century of women', I am one of those who wishes to walk hand in hand, not a step in front or a step behind.

NOIDA
15 August 2014

Rape: Inside the Justice Verma Committee

On Sunday, 23 December 2012, over a quiet lunch at home, a few friends and I were discussing the gang rape that had taken place the previous Sunday and that had triggered widespread outrage around the country. The assault had been horrendous. Five young men and a boy of 17 had gang-raped and brutalized with an iron rod a 23-year-old paramedical student, leaving her for dead before fleeing. The culprits were swiftly apprehended and the facts of the case were reported in great detail in the media.

Accompanied by a male friend, the victim had been making her way home after seeing a movie at about 8.30 in the evening. They had boarded a bus seemingly headed towards their destination. Besides the two of them, the only occupants of the bus were the five men and the boy. As the bus sped down Delhi's ill-lit roads, the young woman was raped repeatedly, and her companion was beaten senseless. After the men finished raping her, an iron rod was used to further brutalize her. The two victims were then thrown out of the bus, nearly dead.

The news of the assault triggered massive, though peaceful, protests by young people, both men and women. People who did not know each other discussed it openly amongst themselves, contacting one another on social media platforms and on other networks. The harrowing ordeal faced by Nirbhaya (or the 'fearless one', as the young woman came to be called by the media, since the law did not permit her real name to be disclosed) and her companion had struck a chord. The authorities were apathetic, but the people wanted the state to enact sterner laws to deal with cases such as these in order to deliver speedier and more effective justice. It was perhaps the first time that young people had engaged in such large-scale spontaneous protests without any organizational involvement of political parties or well-known leaders. The police tried to disperse these demonstrations but the protestors faced water cannons and other forms of intimidation on those cold December mornings. They returned, day after day, to keep up the pressure, and the government was eventually forced to make a commitment to act against sexual violence.

But I am getting ahead of the story. That Sunday, during lunch, my friends were curious about the sort of response I thought the government could be expected to make to the demands of the protestors. My cynical reply was that it would appoint a committee or commission to look into the matter, thus postponing the decision for six months or more, by which time the momentum of the protest would be lost.

Just a few moments later, the then finance minister, Mr P. Chidambaram, telephoned and requested me to be a member of just such a committee! A bit apprehensive, I asked him about the composition of the committee. He told me that it would be headed by Justice J. S. Verma and that its third member would be a senior advocate. I knew Justice Verma to be a fiercely independent and courageous judge and felt it would be a privilege to work with him. I then asked the finance minister when the committee would be expected to table its report. 'Within thirty days,' he replied.

Though I felt strongly about the issue of sexual violence against women and wanted to be a part of an effective committee, I thought it best to decline owing to a previous commitment in Kolkata that overlapped with part of the committee's one-month term. But Mr Chidambaram felt there would be time enough for me to participate in the deliberations of the committee and requested me to agree. In retrospect, I am glad I allowed myself to be persuaded; it was a rare opportunity to work with such an excellent team on such an important issue.

Mr Gopal Subramanium, a former Solicitor General of India and an eminent jurist, was the third member of the committee. He was a whirlwind of energy, and a man of great compassion and learning.

The notification (that formalized the constitution of the committee and its charter) was finalized on the same day, 23 December 2012, and published in the gazette extraordinary under the Ministry of Home Affairs (UT [Union Territory] division) on 24 December 2012. On 25 December a public notice was issued in a number of newspapers requesting people—members of the public, eminent jurists, legal professionals—as well as non-governmental organizations and women's groups to share with the committee their ideas on possible amendments to the relevant laws in order that those accused of sexual assault against women could be quickly tried and appropriately punished.

Though the terms of reference seemed limited to reviewing the law to provide for speedier justice and enhanced punishment in cases of aggravated sexual assault, we knew that we had to come up with a holistic report for it to be meaningful, practical and sound.

At our first meeting on 26 December in Room 222 of the Vigyan Bhavan Annexe, Justice Verma slowly read out a few handwritten paragraphs which he felt could guide us.

> In our present tradition-bound society, structured on the basis of old social values, when a woman is subjected to a crime like rape, it becomes a multiple crime. She is raped at home, then in public life, followed by an agonising cross-examination (by the police and) in the court, and the climax is reached when sensational reports about the crime against her appear in the media. The victim of the crime finds the public exposure more agonising than the crime (of rape) inflicted on her. (It is a continuing rape of her in full public view).
> The (even more) humiliating aspect of the crime against a woman is that her status in the hierarchical structure of society also (obstructs) the way of securing justice for her.
> Thus her social status compounds her gender injustice.

In our present tradition-bound society, structured on the basis of old values, when a woman is subjected to a crime like rape, it becomes a multiple crime. She is raped at home, then in public life, followed by an agonising cross-examination (by the police and) in the court, and the climax is reached when sensational reports about the crime against her appear in the media. The victim of the crime finds public exposure more agonising than the crime (of rape) inflicted on her. (It is a continuing rape of her in full public view).

The (even more) humiliating aspect of the crime against a woman is that her status in the hierarchal structure of society also (obstructs) the way of securing justice for her. Thus, her social status compounds her gender injustice.

In a well-known case, the most obnoxious situation was that the court acquitted the accused, observing that the rapists were middle-aged and respectable of a higher caste who could not commit rape of a lower caste woman. This is the tragedy a woman had to face compounding gender and social injustice.

Every rape, even that by a single individual, is a gang rape and an *aggravated sexual assault*. Taking a holistic view of such a crime, the laws relating to all its aspects must be reviewed for its prevention and punishment. The scrutiny need not be confined only to those laws which relate to the investigation, prosecution and trial of the incident of rape.

We knew that if we waited for the government to provide us with all the facilities we needed, the report would not be completed on time. Gopal put his entire office at our disposal and all his juniors volunteered to help. They roped in others: law students, young lawyers, a law professor. Even Justice Verma's granddaughter, a student at Oxford who was holidaying in India, chipped in. Gopal's trusted junior, Abhishek Tewari, was appointed the committee's counsel and placed in overall organizational charge.

The young team of about sixteen members included four women. They all worked tirelessly, researching and collecting material and also collating the enormous number of suggestions (about 80,000) that poured in from the public. A political party even sent its memorandum of suggestions to Justice Verma's house at 11.45 p.m. on 5 January 2013, fifteen minutes before the deadline, woke him up, and insisted that he personally sign the receipt!

We received advice from experts and academics from abroad, and heard the apprehensions and fears voiced by women's groups, feminists, the lesbian-gay-bisexual-transgender (LGBT) community and many others. We also encouraged the administration and the police to share their points of view. Even though our deadline was long past, the suggestions kept pouring in, and we felt it was important to examine all of them. Thereafter, on Saturday, 19 January and Sunday, 20 January we also held an open hearing in the main hall of Vigyan Bhavan from 9 a.m. to 9 p.m.

As the discussion began, I remember feeling acutely uncomfortable on stage. I am short and, seated on the chair that I was, I could barely reach the table, let alone see over it. My request for a cushion to raise me up was fruitless, as no one could find one in Vigyan Bhavan. During the coffee break, just as I was about to dispatch my driver to go and buy a cushion, someone, having heard of my predicament, pulled a lever under my chair and, magically, the seat shot up.

The discussion was of a high order intellectually, though it was quite emotional. We were especially moved by the stories we heard of rapes in conflict zones, and those committed by the army.

■

Once the hearings were done, it was time to get to work on the final version of the report. We were all very aware that it had to be submitted to the government in the next few days. There were crucial issues which had no ready answers, and were thus hotly debated amongst the team.

On 22 January 2013, a day before we were due to submit our report, we were still debating whether the crime of rape should be gender-neutral or gender-specific. When I had helped draft a bill regarding sexual offences for the 172nd Report of the Law Commission, of which I was a member, we had made rape gender-neutral, which meant that the perpetrator could be 'any person' and the victim could also be 'any person'. This was the modern approach and based on the principle of equality. (This was also the accepted position in Bill No. 130 of 2012, pending in the Lok Sabha.) But there was considerable weight of opinion pressing for this offence to be made gender-specific, that is, the perpetrator should be a man and the victim a woman. After a great deal of brainstorming with our young team we arrived at a consensus: though the perpetrator was identified as a man, the victim was to be categorized as gender-neutral, thus covering males, females, and transgender persons. Professor Mrinal Satish and Shwetasree Majumdar who were helping us draft the bill had to rework it extremely quickly.

The government ordinance issued immediately after our report was submitted kept the offence gender-neutral with regard to both perpetrator and victim, but when the Criminal Law (Amendment) Act, 2013 (hereafter referred to as Act 13 of 2013) was passed by Parliament, it made the offence of rape gender-specific with regard to both perpetrator and victim. It did not accept our in-between position, which effectively extended protection to males and transgenders. In my view this was a serious mistake, and Parliament failed to understand the injustice done thereby to so many men and transgender people.

Another issue was the age categorization of a minor accused in such cases. One of the main offenders in the Nirbhaya case was a 17-year-old, a minor who could be only tried by the Juvenile Justice Board rather than having to undergo the rigour of trial and suffer severe punishment by court. Consequently there was a great deal of debate about categorizing minors as those below the age of 16 rather than the current 18. Though the enactment of a criminal offence is not given retrospective effect and would not have affected the minor accused in Nirbhaya's case, it was argued that a large number of rapes were committed by persons between the ages of 16 and 18 who should be brought within the ambit of the criminal law and punished accordingly.

While we studied this aspect of the matter, we also examined others, such as the neurological state of an adolescent brain, which undergoes significant changes in structure and function during the period of transition to adulthood. This was the reason the US Supreme Court abolished the death penalty for juveniles (*Roper vs Simmons*), holding that retribution is not proportional if the law's most severe penalty is imposed 'on one whose culpability or blameworthiness is diminished, to a substantial degree, by reason of youth and immaturity'.

We also considered the United Nations Convention on the Rights of the Child, and the fact that transformation was hardly likely to take place if juveniles were put into jails with hardened criminals. Further, we considered the fact that recidivism had declined over the years and that children deprived of parental guidance and education had some chance of being rehabilitated if the reformatory system in the juvenile institutions was drastically improved.

Having examined all these aspects, we concluded that no change in the law was required. We recommended that the Juvenile Justice Act be implemented in both letter and spirit. The government accepted this position and the age for minors was not reduced in Act 13 of 2013.

Then came the issue of the extent of punishment. We were against castration or death—which were suggested by various people—as punishments for various reasons detailed in our report. However, our standpoint that even the most grievous offence of rape did not require the imposition of the death penalty was not accepted by the government. We were of the view that punishment for life, meaning the whole of life, would be sufficient and that the punishment of death already existed in the Indian Penal Code in the case of murder. (Nirbhaya had since died in Singapore, where she had been sent by the government for better medical treatment.)

Another hotly debated issue was that of marital rape. This has to be looked at from a historical perspective and the principle of patriarchy. The offence of rape was originally based on the idea of theft of a man's property. According to the old-fashioned notion on which the law was based, a woman belonged first to her father and, after marriage, to her husband. So if anyone had sexual intercourse with her before marriage, the father's honour was affected and, after marriage, the husband's. According to the English common law of coverture, a woman was deemed to have consented at the time of marriage to having intercourse with her husband at his whim. In 1736, Sir Matthew Hale declared that a husband could not be guilty of rape on 'his lawful wife, for by their mutual matrimonial consent and contract' she had agreed to this and this consent 'she cannot retract'.

The situation has changed drastically since then. A woman's autonomy and bodily integrity are concepts that have developed over the years, thus making rape an offence unless there is true consent—not merely consent by legal fiction.

In England in 1991, Lord Keith, speaking for the House of Lords, declared that 'marriage is in modern times regarded as a partnership of equals, and no longer one in which the wife must be the subservient chattel of the husband'. The European Commission of Human Rights also endorsed the conclusion that a rapist remains a rapist regardless of his relationship with the victim. The very essence of the Convention on Human Rights is derived from respect for human rights, dignity and freedom.

In South Africa, marital rape was criminalized in 1993. In Canada, too, it is a crime to rape one's wife. In Australia, in 1991, the common law fiction of irrevocable consent was roundly rejected by Justice Brennan who said it 'has always been offensive to human dignity and incompatible with the legal status of a spouse'. These jurisdictions have also recognized that consent is most important and cannot be implied, and that marital rape cannot be considered a lesser crime with a more lenient sentence.

Consequently we strongly recommended that:

i. the exception for marital rape be removed,

ii. the law ought to specify that:
   a. A marital or other relationship between the perpetrator [and] victim is not a valid defence against the crimes of rape or sexual violation;
   b. The relationship between the accused and the complainant is not relevant to the inquiry into whether the complainant consented to the sexual activity;
   c. The fact that the accused and victim are married or in another intimate relationship may not be regarded as a mitigating factor justifying lower sentences for rape.

Despite our strong recommendation, the government did not agree to make marital rape a crime. Many voices, especially those of men, were raised against it, saying that, if implemented, it would be misused. Another factor that was bandied about was the difficulty of finding evidence of rape in the bedroom—a statement that we found strange, considering that sexual abuse has been defined as an act of domestic violence in the Protection of Women from Domestic Violence Act, 2005. Some people raised the bogey that it would result in the unnecessary break-up of marriages. However, in our view, it would have helped women who needed protection to act against violent husbands. And the police would have been duty-bound to register cases that were reported. Unfortunately the law was not changed by Act 13 of 2013 and the marital exemption has been retained. Exception 2 in Section 375 of the Indian Penal Code reads: 'Sexual intercourse or sexual acts by a man with his own wife, the wife not being under fifteen years of age, is not rape.'

Retaining this exception in spite of our strong recommendation for its removal is unfair to women and violates their dignity and bodily integrity. It is against the spirit of human rights and the Convention on the Elimination of All Forms of Discrimination against Women. Is a woman to be bound by the feudal fiction of irrevocable consent the moment she takes the marriage vows? On the one hand, the government talks of encouraging women, empowering them and enhancing their rights while with the other, it takes away their right to refuse sexual overtures. In this respect the government has failed to do the right thing by women and has been overpowered by patriarchal attitudes.

However, women should not lose heart. Change will come in time, I hope. We need to educate people about the constitutional right of equality. As Professor Sandra Fredman of the University of Oxford said, awareness programmes must be provided to ordinary people so that 'marriage should not be regarded as extinguishing the legal or sexual autonomy of the wife'.

During the course of our discussions, a question arose

about the connection between age and legal consent. According to the law under consideration, a partner under the age of 18 could not be deemed to have given his or her consent. But we felt that adolescent youngsters indulging in teenage romance and consensual sex should not be criminalized, so long as both were at least 16 years of age. Unfortunately, the government did not accept this recommendation either.

While many of our recommendations were not incorporated in Act 13 of 2013, some were, such as those relating to voyeurism and stalking.

We were glad to note that an acid attack (throwing or administering acid) had been included as a specific crime in Bill No. 130 of 2012. We had heard horrible stories of how a man would stalk a woman and if she objected to or turned down his advances would throw acid on her face, thus not only causing her unbearable physical agony but also permanently destroying her self-worth and esteem, causing her permanent physical damage and completely ruining her life. Consequently, we felt that this might have been averted if stalking were clearly an offence. It would also ensure the security and safety of women.

So who is a stalker? He has been defined as 'any man who follows a woman and contacts, or attempts to contact such woman to foster personal interaction repeatedly despite a clear indication of disinterest by such woman'. The law provides that this monitoring by a man can also be by use of the internet, email or any other form of electronic communication. Our recommendation to impose a punishment of three years in jail and a fine was accepted.

■

On the night of 22 January 2013, Justice Verma and I left at midnight, while Gopal and the young team worked through the night, incorporating corrections and changes into the report. It was only a few minutes before 7 a.m. on the morning of 23 January that Abhishek Tewari telephoned Justice Verma to tell him that work on the report was complete. It was then sent to the printer. A hardbound copy was produced before us at 12.30 p.m. and the three of us signed it with Gopal's Mont Blanc pen. It was then sent to the prime minister with a covering letter which expressed our hope that there would be speedy implementation of our recommendations 'to retain public confidence in good governance'. Prime Minister Manmohan Singh thanked us for our labour of love and assured us that the government would 'be prompt in pursuing the recommendations of the Committee'.

Though an ordinance and then the Act were passed promptly, many of our other suggestions, including those pertaining to Police Reforms, the Representation of the People Act, 1951, the Armed Forces (Special Powers) Act, 1958, and the Women's Charter, as well as various recommendations relating to awareness and education in order to help change the patriarchal mindset of the country are still to be implemented.

There was a grim sense of justice achieved when all

the surviving adult men accused of raping and murdering Nirbhaya (one of them committed suicide in his jail cell) were convicted and sentenced to death. The sentence was upheld by the High Court, but the accused appealed to the Supreme Court and have obtained a stay of execution. However, there was outrage when the juvenile offender was let off with a mere three years incarceration in a reform home.

Women continue to be raped almost daily, if the reports in the newspapers are anything to go by, and the great swell of outrage that accompanied the tragic death of a brave young woman would seem to have achieved almost nothing at all. It would be easy to be disheartened by all this. But I am not. A real beginning was made when tens of thousands of people came together and demanded concrete action from government and the authorities. The 631-page report that we prepared in just twenty-nine days has led to some changes that I believe will, in time, lead to far-reaching improvements in the lives of the women of this country. And it is not only I who think this. Let the last words in this essay go to a representative of this country's young women, who will effect and be affected by the change that I am positive will come. She is Shwetasree Majumder (an intellectual property lawyer and the general secretary of the Society of Women Lawyers) who assisted us on the report and later, in her blog on NDTV, shared her experience of working with the committee. (I quote her, needless to say, not for her generous encomia but because she conveys a vivid sense of the atmosphere in which we all worked.) She writes:

> I don't think any of us had quite fathomed what we were getting into. Hot-blooded, raring to go, willing to be part of a change that we hoped would last, the answer on each of our lips was 'Yes', when we were asked if we would help the Verma Committee. And then it hit us. 80,000 emails, the phone ringing off the hook and 14 perplexed lawyers, one historian/sociologist and one law student—we had clearly bitten off way more than we could chew.
>
> Interestingly, the one thing that held us together was neither similar thinking nor synchronized working styles—it was humour! And once that clicked it was a cakewalk. Through the endless cups of tea and the now-legendary heart-shaped cutlets in the Vigyan Bhavan Annexe to hurling imaginary offences and penalties at each other, we used humour to stay upbeat, positive and optimistic...
>
> The biggest motivation however, was the Committee itself. The ever smiling octogenarian at the helm of it (he celebrated his 80th birthday in Vigyan Bhavan eating those very heart-shaped cutlets) whose patience and broad outlook were truly worthy of respect. From lowering the age of consent to 16, to including all persons in the ambit of sexual assault, to including hate crimes like female genital mutilation within the scope of the new spectrum of offences —Justice Verma's vision should be lauded as being in

perfect tandem with the modern world.

Justice Leila Seth has been a long time inspiration—once again another liberal and an incredibly humble one. Despite deep reserves of specific knowledge on the subject (having co-authored the Law Commission's 172nd Report which reviewed rape laws) she did not approach the subject with any preconceived notions and was always willing to give every one of our views a patient ear and vote for adopting the approach that sounded most fair.

And finally, to use Justice Verma's words, the 'youngest member of the committee', Mr Subramani[u]m, who also celebrated his 30th wedding anniversary in these few [manic] days by acknowledging that his wife deserved better! I cannot name anyone, far less a senior counsel who would put his extremely lucrative practice completely on hold for a whole month to throw himself, heart and soul, into a social cause the way he did. From giving each one of us unfettered access to his office, his resources and his staff, to sitting with us shoulder-to-shoulder and burning the midnight oil and then working on his own long after we were gone (until he actually crashed out in the middle of the day from sheer exhaustion—but only once!), from giving everyone who walked in through the doors of his office offering valuable information to assist the committee a patient ear, to sifting through absolute mountains of material to find the nerve of every issue, he was like a man possessed. And with these three incredible human beings steering the ship, it was of no surprise that something powerful was born...

It falls to me to add a sad addendum to this account. Barely three months after the report was produced and published, Justice J. S. Verma died.

This was a real tragedy. The only consolation is that, like a true karmayogi, he was able to work till the last, so indefatigably, so unsparingly and so humanely, for a cause that may do so much good for so many.

Gender Sensitization of the Judiciary

Bhanwari Devi was a saathin (grass-roots worker) in a village called Bhateri, Rajasthan, who was working under the Women's Development Programme of the Rajasthan state government. She carried out a vigorous campaign against the evil of child marriage. When she succeeded in preventing the marriage of the one-year-old daughter of Ram Karan Gujjar, she was allegedly gang-raped by five men on 22 September 1992. The victim's efforts to seek justice were futile because it appeared that the culprits could influence the local police. Her medical examination was delayed.

The National Commission for Women, at the request of a voluntary organization, visited the village to investigate the case. They held discussions with medical experts, police officers and officers of the Women's Development Programme. They met the chief minister and asked him to take stringent action. Women's organizations were naturally agitated about the inertia of the state law enforcement machinery and the efforts to shield the culprits. The commission took up the matter with the union home minister and the minister of Human Resource Development. On the basis of the commission's report, a sum of ₹10,000 was sanctioned from the Prime Minister's Relief Fund to the victim. Subsequently, the case was entrusted to the Central Bureau of Investigation and a case registered. The District and Sessions Court, Jaipur, acquitted the accused in this case.

What is historic, however, is the view taken by the judge that the accused, by virtue of their age and social standing, were necessarily incapable of a crime like rape. The judgment suggests that rapists are usually teenagers. This may or may not be statistically true, but extending that to mean that all those who are not teenagers cannot rape is ludicrous. If this were to be accepted, all cases of rape should be dropped the moment it is established that the accused have crossed their teens. Equally astonishing is the claim that since the alleged rapists were middle-aged they must necessarily be 'respectable', a contention supported neither by statistics nor by elementary logic.

The most astounding reason given for acquittal, however, was that the accused (one of whom was a Brahmin) were fairly highly placed in the caste hierarchy, and that this ruled them out as possible rapists of a lower-caste woman. Such caste characterization of crime, apart from being morally objectionable, betrays an entirely ahistorical perspective. And this perspective, while insidious in society at large, is even more abhorrent within the judiciary.

Women in India normally exist either as a part of their parents' or their husbands' homes. After their husbands die, they live in their sons' homes, dependent on them. Consequently, their freedom and equality are dependent on the attitudes of these families, who normally treat them as subservient. The question of independence and of having a home of their own, where they can live as they would wish to, rarely arises. But equality is what they are entitled to and what they should receive.

The Indian Constitution has clearly indicated that equality is a fundamental right. Article 14 guarantees equality before the law and equal protection under the law. Article 15 prohibits discrimination on the grounds of religion, race, caste, sex and place of birth, and Article 15(3) permits the state to make special provision for women. Article 16 provides for equality of opportunity in matters of public employment.

Equality is not defined and is perhaps undefinable. Equality means different things at different times and to different people. But in law there is a formal approach, that is, those similarly situated are to be treated equally; further, one cannot treat unequals as equal. So if persons are different then differential treatment is justified. But substantive equality requires that inequality of disadvantaged groups in society be eliminated. How is this change to be brought about—by reservation? The dilemma is that reservations violate equality in that everybody is not treated equally; but at the same time reservations could be fundamental to equality since bringing about equality might require disadvantaged groups to be treated advantageously. But will reservations result in equality or perpetuate a disadvantaged group—one that will become dependent on its crutches?

Constitutional law and Supreme Court judgments hold that equality does not require the law to treat all individuals in the same manner. But if classifications are made between individuals, these should be reasonable, that is, founded on 'intelligible differentia' and that such differentia must have a 'rational relation' to the object sought to be achieved.

The approach normally taken with gender equality is that women are different from men because they are weaker and subordinate and consequently need protection. Women are basically thought of as wives and mothers and as such allocated the role and responsibility of looking after the home and the children. Because of this role they are economically dependent on men. But the protectionist approach reinforces this difference and perpetuates it. On the other hand, taking into consideration the fact that women bear children, an attempt must be made to examine the difficulties faced by women because of this difference and to give them special treatment. That is, a working woman must be given proper and adequate maternity leave and not penalized (by witholding promotions) for this, thus treating her on par with her male colleagues. This compensatory approach acknowledges that pregnancy, childbearing and taking care of a small child make a woman's life different and this difference must be clearly recognized and its relevance acknowledged. Thus, this historically disadvantaged group needs compensatory and corrective treatment, because failure to appreciate the difference only serves to reinforce and perpetuate the differences and not improve the position of women.

As judges and lawyers, we are required to do justice, and justice requires an even hand. Without equality there is no justice. Justice has to be done without fear or favour, affection or ill-will or taking into consideration such factors as race, caste, sex, etc. In a model society one would expect every individual to have equal opportunity and equal chances and be able to lead a life of dignity so that one can realize his/her aspirations.

With all the historical baggage we carry, it is difficult to understand and appreciate the meaning of true equality. We face difficulties because there are no definite parameters. What might have looked just and fair a century ago in the manner of the treatment of women no longer looks just and fair. In 1916, Regina Guha, a young woman in Calcutta, was refused the right to practise law on the grounds that women were not fit for the 'hurly burly of the legal profession'. Similarly, in 1921, Sudhansu Bala Hazra was refused permission in Patna as it was considered repugnant to ideas of decorum to permit women to join in the 'rough and tumble of the forensic arena'. But today there are women in the legal profession both as practising lawyers and as judges, though the number of women judges is comparatively low. There are presently two women out of thirty judges in the Supreme Court; there are about sixty women judges out of approximately 650 women judges in the High Courts and a small percentage in the subordinate judiciary.

However, there cannot be any hard and fast rule; it is a matter of approach. We as lawyers and judges have to think equality before we can write equality. Writing judgments is an art, but the thought process behind it involves our background and upbringing. And if this thought process or language of the mind is outdated, we have to re-educate ourselves. The forces that make us what we are lie in our consciousness. The way your father treated your mother or how they dealt with you and your siblings when you were young are all part of that consciousness. But so is the way that you treat your mother, wife or daughter. And if you are made aware that you don't treat them fairly or equally, you can try and learn the language of equality. As Gandhiji said, 'Every home is a university and the parents are the teachers'.

Since the law is constantly changing, the knowledge of law requires constant refreshing. Similarly, attitudes and approaches that influenced one's youth also have to be re-examined. The importance of this continuous process of re-educating oneself cannot be overestimated. The function of the judiciary is to provide justice. How do we educate and re-educate ourselves to be good judges—judges to whom integrity and impartiality and a judicious temperament are of paramount importance? A judge is always on display and it is not only his judgments but his manner of dealing with the public and people that is important. He has to conduct himself with dignity and decorum and without prejudice. There can be no dichotomy in his thought process while writing judgments and in his conduct and reactions outside court. He must recognize women's rights in court, in the world at large, and at home.

A judge, in his dealings with the public, has to be doubly careful, particularly circumspect, because, like Caesar's wife, no one should be able to point a finger at him. The public usually first comes in contact with a magistrate or subordinate judge and that is the impression of the judiciary which they carry. For instance, when I was appointed a judge of the Delhi High Court in 1978, my neighbour asked me whether the judicial magistrate of the area was my boss. 'He is all-powerful,' she said. The subordinate judge or magistrate is the most visible rung of the judiciary and the one with which the public is most concerned. So his attitudes are most important.

Once a matter has been heard in court, the judge has to take a decision after assessing the arguments and the position of the various parties. The ultimate decision is contained in the judgment. Lord Macmillan observed: 'It is a reasoned pronouncement by a judge on a disputed legal question which has been argued before him... The judge speaks with authority and what he says should therefore be spoken with befitting dignity. He should not affect a grand eloquence but he has to be impressive. The strength of a judgment lies in its reasoning and it should therefore be convincing. Clarity of exposition is always essential. Dignity, convincingness and clarity are exacting requirements but they are subservient to what, after all, is the main object of a judgment, which is not only to do but to be seen to do justice.' In writing a judgment, first the material facts have to be marshalled in a logical way, leaving out the inessential. The next step is to formulate and apply the law to them. This generally involves a critical examination of principles and precedents and is the core of the judgment. The conclusion follows.

It all sounds very simple, but is an extremely exacting exercise because, in order to do it well, one has to master the facts and the law. The fact finder's perceptions and prejudices affect the decision. The judge has to be sensitive to the realities in the context of each case and should not be influenced by his own predilections. Objectivity is needed in order to ensure equality. Equality will be a hollow concept if it is subordinated to every other value that a court feels is constitutionally pressing. It is important to have equality without discrimination, as they are inextricably linked. As Justice Claire L'Heureux Dubé of Canada has observed:

> Equality is not simply about equal treatment, and it is not a mathematical equation waiting to be solved. It is about human dignity and full membership in society. It is about promoting an equal sense of self-worth. It is about treating people with equal concern, equal respect and equal consideration. *Those* are the values

that underlie equality. Those are the values that are offended when we discriminate, consciously or not.

It appears to me that the manner in which a judge treats a woman lawyer, a woman petitioner, a woman respondent or a woman witness, and his attitude in trying to understand the problems of a woman litigant together with his dealings with the female members of his own family and those of his friends and acquaintances, all add up to the sum total of his approach to gender, his objectivity and his sense of fairness. Because that is what equality and justice are all about. As Lord Diplock said, 'Law is about man's duty to his neighbour'. And I would add that the neighbour's gender should not make any difference.

I think that everyone agrees that integrity and impartiality are the essential qualities of a judge. That is why the judge's oath says that one must decide without fear or favour, affection or ill-will. Lord Devlin, speaking of race relations, said that the social service which judges rendered was the removal of a sense of injustice and for this both impartiality and the appearance of impartiality were essential. This can truly be said with regard to cases pertaining to women and the girl child.

It is clear that the judicial function is not automatic and that therefore it is necessary to recommend and train intellectually able men and women to serve as judges who will decide cases as objectively as possible. Judicial independence means that judges are not dependent on governments in ways which might influence them in coming to a decision in individual cases. But judges are human and have human prejudices. A judge is conscious that his reputation as a judge is likely to be adversely affected if he decides one way and favourably affected if he decides another way. Such pressures do exist. Judges are the product of a class and have characteristics of that class dependent on the family they belong to and school and university they attended. As such, there is a difference in perception and perspective between the lower and the higher judiciary.

This difference is clearly illustrated by various decisions of the courts. The sensitivity displayed by the Supreme Court of India in rape cases is often lacking in judgments of the trial courts. This is a disquieting and disturbing fact.

In *State of Punjab vs Gurmit Singh and Others,* where the charge was of abduction and rape of a young girl of 16, the trial court acquitted the accused. Dr Justice A. S. Anand, speaking for the Supreme Court of India observed in paragraphs 13, 14 and 15 of his judgment:

13. The trial Court not only erroneously disbelieved the prosecutrix, but quite uncharitably and unjustifiably even characterised her as a girl 'of loose morals' or 'such type of a girl'.

14. What has shocked our judicial conscience all the more is the inference drawn by the Court, based on no evidence and not even on a denied suggestion, to the effect:

'The more probability is that (prosecutrix) was a girl of loose character. She wanted to dupe her parents that she resided for one night at the house of her maternal uncle, but for the reasons best known to her, she does not do so and she preferred to give company to some persons.'

15. We must express our strong disapproval of the approach of the trial court and its casting a stigma on the character of the prosecutrix. The observations lack sobriety expected of a Judge. Such like stigmas have the potential of not only discouraging an even otherwise reluctant victim of sexual assault to bring forth complaint for trial of criminals, thereby making the society to suffer by letting the criminal escape even a trial. The Courts are expected to use self-restraint while recording such findings which have larger repercussions so far as the future of the victim of the sex crime is concerned and even wider implications on the society as a whole—where the victim of crime is discouraged—the criminal encouraged and in turn crime gets rewarded. Even in cases unlike the present case, where there is some acceptable material on the record to show that the victim was habituated to sexual intercourse, no such inference like the victim being a girl of 'loose moral character' is permissible to be drawn from that circumstance alone. Even if the prosecutrix

in a given case has been promiscuous in her sexual behaviour earlier, she has a right to refuse to submit herself to sexual intercourse to anyone and everyone because she is not a vulnerable object or prey for being sexually assaulted by anyone and everyone. No stigma, like the one as cast in the present case should be cast against such a witness by the Courts, for after all it is the accused and not the victim of sex crime who is on trial in the Court.

After convicting the accused, the Supreme Court observed that such matters must be handled with the utmost sensitivity. I can do no better than quote the words of the learned judge, Dr Justice A. S. Anand: 'A murderer destroys the physical body of his victim, a rapist degrades the very soul of the helpless female. The courts, therefore, shoulder a greater responsibility while trying an accused on charges of a rape.'

Let us compare these sentiments above with those of the District and Sessions Judge, Jaipur, who decided Bhanwari Devi's case. The case of Bhanwari Devi illustrates how the prejudices of a judge are displayed in a judgment.

An editorial in the *Pioneer* on 27 November 1995 called the Bhanwari Devi judgment morally repugnant and agreed that the righteous indignation of women's organizations was not misplaced. On the contrary, it would be surprising if the sensibilities of right-minded and responsible citizens had not been hurt by this judgment. 'The track record of India's judicial system in dispensing justice in rape cases has been anything but exemplary. To that extent, the acquittal of the five persons accused of having gang-raped the saathin working with the Women's Development Programme of Rajasthan is by itself neither historic nor even remarkable. If anything, it only further underlines the fact that rape victims in this country have only a faint hope of seeing justice being done.'

Such a judgment would have been reprehensible in any rape case, but the specific circumstances of this case make it more so. What is alleged in this case is not just that Ms Devi was raped to satiate a few men's lust but that humiliation was inflicted upon her because of her campaign against child marriage, which went against the feudal set-up. It is therefore of paramount importance that justice be done and be seen to be done. It remains the duty of the judiciary and the state to ensure that this does happen. If not, others working for social reforms may well lose heart and begin to believe that they are not only fighting the feudal order but also a supposedly modern state.

This case raises many questions: How does an international covenant like the Convention on the Elimination of All Forms of Discrimination against Women (CEDAW) help the Bhanwari Devis of this world? How can one prevent violence, especially the terrible trauma of rape, being used against women? How can one prevent harassment of this nature of a person who is doing her work conscientiously? How can feudal attitudes be changed so that discrimination and domination ends? Where are equality and justice, development and peace?

Gender sensitization of the judiciary is essential. Members of the judiciary must be made aware of international conventions like CEDAW and the Declaration on the Elimination of Violence against Women. A study done by the NGO Sakshi in 1996 found that most judges were not even aware of these conventions or declarations and that 64 per cent of them felt that women must share the blame for violence committed against them.

We have to strengthen international accountability; make provision for advisory services with adequate funding; improve the efficiency of the review bodies; bring about increased awareness of human rights through information and education; establish national institutions for the promotion and protection of rights; and make the interflow between international and domestic law more effective.

Justice J. S. Verma, speaking for the Supreme Court in *Vishakha vs State of Rajasthan* (a public interest litigation which was filed by Vishakha, a women's organization, and others in the Supreme Court after the Bhanwari Devi case in order to enforce the fundamental rights of working women) has held that it is now an accepted rule of judicial construction that regard must be paid to international conventions and norms for construing domestic law when there is no inconsistency between them and where there is a void in the domestic law.

In fact, the court was of the opinion that in the absence of domestic law occupying the field, it was necessary to formulate effective measures to check the evil of sexual harassment of working women at all workplaces. As such, the contents of international conventions and norms are significant for the purpose of interpreting the guarantees of gender equality, right to work and human dignity as provided for in Articles 14, 15, 19 (1) (g) and 21 of the Constitution and the safeguards against sexual harassment implicit therein. It was further of the view that any international convention not inconsistent with the fundamental rights and in harmony with it must be read into these provisions to enlarge the meaning and content thereof and to promote the object of the constitutional guarantees. This is implicit from Article 51 and the enabling power of Parliament to enact laws for implementing the international conventions and norms by virtue of Article 253 read with Entry 14 of the Union List in the Seventh Schedule of the Constitution.

The court set out the guidelines pertaining to sexual harassment at the workplace in the judgment that came to be known as the Vishakha Guidelines and were to be in force until a specific law was enacted. This law—the Sexual Harassment of Women in the Workplace (Prevention, Prohibition and Redressal) Act, 2013 was only enacted sixteen years later.

As is apparent from what is outlined above, the Supreme Court of India is trying to teach a new language of equality and bring about a change in the consciousness of the lower judiciary, employers and others.

Lord Justice Scrutton said, 'The habits you are trained in, the people with whom you mix, lead to your having a certain class of ideas of such a nature that, when you have to deal with other ideas, you do not give as sound and accurate judgments as you would wish'. That is why one group of people with certain commitments can say to another group: 'Where are your impartial Judges? They all move in the same circles as the employers and they are all educated and nursed in the same ideas as the employers. How can a labour man or a trade unionist get impartial justice?' Consequently, it is clear that it is very difficult 'to be sure that you have put yourself into a thoroughly impartial position between two disputants, one of your own class and one not of your class'. This could easily be read as one of your own gender and one not of your gender. In a country where a woman is raped every twenty minutes and one is murdered for dowry every sixty minutes, impartiality in decision-making is absolutely essential.

So can a woman get impartial justice from a man? Or, conversely, can a man get impartial justice from a woman? The answer is yes—in both cases. But judges have to learn the language of equality and impartiality. They have to place themselves alternately in the shoes of the two disputants and appreciate the problem before giving an objective decision. This process of learning the language of equality is slow, but it must be continuously engaged in and encouraged. This can be done through discussions, refresher courses, workshops, debates, advocacy and education. Otherwise there will be no equality and no justice. Just as one learns a new language when one goes to a new country, so must we learn the language of equality in the hope and with the desire to eliminate injustice.

Social Action Litigation

Social action litigation or public interest litigation, as it is better known, can be described as an experiment in finding ways and means to overcome the bias of the legal system against the poor and disadvantaged. However, it demands more than righteous indignation. Objectivity, forensic skill, procedural gamesmanship and socio-legal perception are all required.

Public interest law became well known as a concept during the 1960s in the United States of America. It referred to the activities of a group of young lawyers who represented clients and took on causes previously unchampioned in the courts. These creative lawyers filed test cases and class action suits challenging discriminatory laws and promoting the cause and the values of the civil rights movement. They dealt with a wide range of topical issues, including social exploitation, discrimination, environmental pollution, consumer protection and violations of anti-trust laws.

In India, the first seeds of public interest litigation were sown by certain Supreme Court judges who believed in and developed the ideology behind it. Many of the other judges were apprehensive about this new role of assertive activism, preferring to stick to their traditional role of umpiring. Justice V. R. Krishna Iyer, however, was among those who championed judicial activism as essential if justice were to become a reality for the person on the street. He held that Article 39A of the Directive Principles of State Policy, which places a duty on the state to secure equal justice and free legal aid, can be used to interpret Articles 14 and 21 of the Indian Constitution which protect the fundamental rights to equality and to life. This decision is remarkable because the Directive Principles of State Policy, which form a separate part of the Indian Constitution, are in Article 37, expressly made non-enforceable by the courts.

Similarly, in *Hussainara Khatoon and Others vs Home Secretary, State of Bihar*, Justice P. N. Bhagwati observed that the powers of the Supreme Court in protecting constitutional rights are very broad. There was therefore no reason why the Supreme Court should not adopt an activist approach and issue directives to the state. The directive in this case obliged the state to take positive action to secure the fundamental right to a speedy trial. Justice Bhagwati held that an unduly delayed trial is not one based on a just and reasonable procedure.

This case arose from a newspaper report which alleged that a number of prisoners in the state of Bihar had been awaiting trial for between three and ten years without any commencement of proceedings against them. Justice Bhagwati held that it was a travesty of justice that many poor accused were forced into 'long cellular servitude' because bail was beyond their meagre means, and trials 'do not commence, and even if they do, they never conclude'. In fact, it was found that some of the prisoners awaiting trial had been in jail for periods longer than the maximum term to which they could have been sentenced if convicted. The court held that their detention was illegal as it was in violation of the fundamental right to liberty contained in Article 21 of the Constitution, and it ordered their immediate release.

During the course of the hearing it also became apparent that some of the women being held in jail were not accused of any offence at all. Rather, they were in 'protective custody' as victims of or witnesses to offences, and were required to give evidence for the state. Justice Bhagwati declared that 'protective custody' was no more than a euphemism calculated to disguise the reality of imprisonment. Women kept in jail under the guise of 'protective custody' suffered involuntary deprivation of their liberty for long periods through no fault of their own. Moreover, no provision in Indian law permitted the holding of witnesses in protective custody.

The court went on to observe that the government of a social welfare state was obliged to set up rescue and welfare homes to take care of women and children who had nowhere else to go and who were otherwise uncared for by society. It was part of the duty of government to protect the homeless and destitute, and it was surprising that the government of Bihar attempted to justify keeping women in 'protective custody' on the grounds that a welfare home maintained by the state had been shut down. The Supreme Court duly directed that all women and children kept in jail in the state of Bihar under 'protective custody' or as witnesses in forthcoming trials should be released forthwith and properly accommodated and cared for in welfare or rescue homes.

This was an epoch-making decision, not least because it dealt with the duty of the state to provide legal aid to the poor in criminal cases. The court used Article 39A of the Directive Principles to guide its interpretation of Article 21 of the Indian Constitution. The court held that it was not enough to have some semblance of procedure. Rather, the procedure under which a person might be deprived of life or liberty had to be 'reasonable, fair and just'. A procedure which failed to make legal representation available to accused persons unable to afford such a service could not be regarded as 'reasonable, fair and just'.

In *Municipal Council, Ratlam vs Vardhichand and Others,* the Supreme Court upheld the right of residents in a certain area to initiate proceedings to compel the municipality to provide sanitary facilities. Justice Krishna Iyer observed:

> At issue is the coming of age of that brand of public law bearing on community actions and the court's power to force public bodies, under public duties, to implement specific plans in response to public grievances.

In *People's Union for Democratic Rights vs Union of India*

and Others Justice Bhagwati dealt at some length with the scope and nature of public interest litigation and the importance of its role in ensuring the protection of the basic human rights of the poor and weaker sections of the community. The main thrust of his reasoning as contained in Paragraphs 2 and 3 is summarized below:

> Public interest litigation, a strategic arm of the legal aid movement, which is intended to bring justice within the reach of the poor masses, is fundamentally different from traditional litigation, which is adversarial in character. Public interest litigation does not seek to enforce the right of one individual against another. Rather, public interest cases are brought before the courts to promote and vindicate the public interest which demands that legal remedies be available for violations of the constitutional or legal rights of poor and disadvantaged communities. Failure to provide such redress would be destructive of the rule of law, which is an essential element of democratic forms of government. The rule of law demands that the protection of the law is available to every citizen. The law should not be allowed to uphold the status quo by protecting the vested interests of a fortunate few under the guise of securing their civil and political rights.
>
> Public interest litigation is essentially a cooperative or collaborative effort on the part of the petitioner, the state or public authority, and the court. Its aim is to ensure that the constitutional or legal rights, benefits

and privileges established in a society are, in fact, available to all members of that society, irrespective of their social or economic position. Thus, the respondent in public interest litigation, be it the state or a public authority, should have as great an interest in ensuring basic human rights—particularly in respect to the poor and vulnerable—as the petitioner. Correctly approached, public interest litigation offers the state an opportunity to right a wrong or redress an injustice. As such, it should be perceived as a mechanism to assist the state in achieving social objectives.

However, public interest litigation is misconstrued by some lawyers, journalists and others in public life as unnecessarily adding to the burdens of an administrative justice system that is already sorely stretched. While it is true that there is an immense backlog of cases, this is no reason for denying the poor and vulnerable access to justice. The time has come for the courts to shed their role as upholders of the establishment, and become champions of the rights of the poor and struggling masses to whom justice has been denied by a cruel and heartless society for generations. It is, in fact, public interest litigation that is responsible for an increasing focus on the problems of the poor which are, in the end, the problems of the whole society. Not only is this kind of litigation changing the entire theatre of the law, it also holds out hope for the future.

The *People's Union for Democratic Rights* case, which elicited this judicial passion, arose out of the allegation that contract labourers employed by the state to construct roads, stadiums, swimming pools and so on for the Asian Games were being exploited. It emerged that, in contravention of a minimum wage stipulation of ₹9.25 a day, male labourers were being paid ₹8.25. Moreover, female labourers were being paid only ₹7 a day, in violation of the Equal Remuneration Act, 1976. The difference between the wages of male and female labourers was being pocketed as commission by the person acting as middleman between the migrant construction workers and the contractor to whom the state contract had been awarded.

Noting that the respondent had launched a number of prosecutions in relation to violations of labour laws, Justice Bhagwati suggested that in future, when contracts were awarded by the government or governmental authority, such authority should assume two responsibilities. First, it should ensure that wages were paid by the contractor to the workers directly, without the intervention of any middleman. Second, it should take steps to ensure that the provisions of the labour laws were strictly observed.

The judge also made certain pertinent observations about the meaning of 'traffic in human beings' and other forms of forced labour which are prohibited by Article 23 of the Indian Constitution. He said it was not only physical force that might compel a person to provide labour or service to another on exploitative terms. Hunger and poverty, want and destitution could also operate as compulsions.

It is clear from this decision and the others noted above that judicial activism was being established as an agency of reform and that at least part of the Supreme Court Bench was attempting to ensure that the poor and disadvantaged were not excluded from enjoyment of the rights guaranteed by the Indian Constitution. Such judicial activism has also been apparent in cases pertaining specifically to women, the majority of whom, in India as elsewhere, constitute the most disadvantaged sector of society.

In 1983, journalist and social activist Sheela Barse wrote a letter to the Supreme Court complaining that women held in police cells in Bombay were being assaulted and tortured. The court viewed this letter as a petition and called upon the state and the Inspector General of Prisons to reply. It directed a social worker to visit the jail and consult privately with the women concerned in order to determine the veracity of the allegations and report back to the court.

In consequence, the court reiterated the duty of the state to provide legal representation to poor or indigent accused, a duty imposed not only by Article 39A of the Directive Principles but also by Articles 14 and 21 of the Indian Constitution. In addition, noting that there had been 'meaningful and constructive debate' before it, and also that the state of Maharashtra had 'offered its full cooperation to the court in laying down the guidelines which should be followed so far as women prisoners in police lock-ups are concerned', the court issued a number of directions.

First, the court ordered the designation of a number of lock-ups where only female suspects should be kept and where the guards should also be female. Second, interrogation of female suspects should take place only in the presence of female police officers. Third, the court ordered that those arrested without a warrant should be informed immediately both of the grounds for their arrest and of their right to apply for bail. In addition, the Maharashtra State Board of Legal Aid and Advice was to print a pamphlet, in the three main languages spoken in the state, setting out the legal rights of arrested persons. The court ordered that copies of the pamphlet should be put up in each cell in every police lock-up and that the pamphlet should also be read, in the appropriate language, to arrested persons on their arrival at the police station.

The court ordered, furthermore, that the police should inform the nearest Legal Aid Committee of all arrests and that such committee should take immediate steps to provide legal assistance to those arrested. Funds for this purpose should be provided to the committee by the state government. In addition, the police should inform a relative or friend designated by an arrested person of the fact of his or her arrest.

Another directive was that the principal judge of Bombay's City Civil Court should designate a judge, preferably a woman, to make periodic surprise visits to police lock-ups in the city. The purpose of such visits would be to ascertain police compliance with the law and directives from the court, and also to allow arrested persons an opportunity to air grievances. Mechanisms for dealing with any lapses by the police in this regard formed part of the directive.

Finally, the court ordered that the magistrate before whom an arrested person was produced should inquire whether such person had any complaint of torture or maltreatment during custody, and inform him of his right to be medically examined.

I have detailed the directions of the court to illustrate two points: first, the type of relief an activist court ordered for the assistance of the helpless and, second, the fact that this relief was the result of cooperation between the Bench, the Bar and government authorities.

In *Upendra Baxi and Others vs State of Uttar Pradesh and Others*, a letter written in 1981 by two law professors complaining about the inhuman and undignified conditions suffered by inmates of the Agra Protective Home for Women was entertained as a writ petition. The court made a number of orders aimed at ensuring a decent and healthy standard of living for the women, and asked the district judge to make periodic inspections with a view to monitoring full and effective implementation of the orders. However, improvements resulting from the court's intervention were set at naught by the state government, which relocated the home to a poorly constructed building in a lonely and distant place.

The Supreme Court accordingly issued further directions with respect to the new site, including improvements to the approach road to the building, installation of more windows for proper cross-ventilation, provision of cooking gas, mosquito nets and safe electricity, and also provision of police protection and transport. Furthermore, the court reiterated its earlier directions regarding formulation and implementation of a rehabilitation programme aimed at helping the inmates to become self-sufficient, so that economic want would not compel them into prostitution when they left the home. Finally, the court ordered that a Board of Visitors should be constituted, as prescribed in Rule 40 of the rules made under the Suppression of Immoral Traffic in Women and Girls Act of 1956, and that the board should include at least three social activists working in this field. The district judge was also directed to nominate two socially committed advocates to provide inmates of the home with legal aid and assistance.

Another example of this kind of judicial intervention arose from a letter written to Justice Bhagwati by social worker Chinnamma Shiv Das. Treated as a writ petition, the letter complained of horrifying conditions at Nari Niketan, a rescue home for women in Delhi. One of the problems mentioned was that the women were not supplied with sanitary napkins during their menses, and the court immediately directed that these be supplied.

The evils of the dowry system, which continue unabated although condemned by many people, has also been the subject of social action litigation. Women's organizations have filed cases asking the courts to use their constitutional power to intervene in and expedite investigations into cases of harassment and death associated with dowry practices. In *Joint Women's Programme vs State of Rajasthan and Others*, the court ordered that cases of death associated with dowry should be investigated by a police officer not lower in rank than a superintendent of police. Where investigations had been conducted by an officer of lower rank, a superintendent of police should 'give a fresh look to the whole matter' and proceed with the investigation without being inhibited by the view taken by the subordinate officer. The court also ordered the states of Rajasthan and Haryana to create a special unit at the state level to investigate dowry deaths. It further directed that a number of women social workers should be nominated by the Ministry of Social Welfare and Women to work in association with such dowry investigation units.

In 1989, Pratul Kumar Sinha, an advocate from Nadia in West Bengal, wrote a letter to the Supreme Court drawing its attention to a newspaper report alleging sexual exploitation of blind girls at a school in the state of Orissa. The letter was registered as a writ petition and the Supreme Court directed the chief judicial magistrate of the area to inquire into the allegations and submit a report. His report indicated that, although there was a lurking suspicion that one of the girls may have been sexually exploited, it was difficult to be certain beyond doubt. However, there was no question of rampant or widespread exploitation of the blind girls. Consequently, the court confined itself to issuing certain directions regarding the management of the institution for blind girls.

In 1990, Gaurav Jain, also an advocate, filed a public interest petition in the Supreme Court seeking an order requiring the Union of India and other respondents to provide separate schools with vocational training and hostels for the children of prostitutes. However, the court was of the view that segregating prostitutes' children in separate schools and hostels was not in the interest of the children. Nevertheless, the children of prostitutes, particularly girl children, should not, the court stated, be exposed to the undesirable environment of prostitution, and therefore accommodation in hostels and reformatories should be made available to help segregate these children from their mothers. The court noted that, despite legislation aimed at controlling the problem of prostitution, it was on the increase and required serious and effective attention. The Supreme Court therefore constituted a committee to examine and report on the problems of prostitutes and rehabilitation of their children, directing the Union of India to deposit ₹20,000 to meet the expenses of this inquiry.

Problems relating to prostitution were the subject of another social action case, again brought by an advocate by means of a letter to the Supreme Court. The court summarized the problem stated in the writ petition of Vishal Jeet as follows:

Many unfortunate teenaged female children…and girls in full bloom are being sold in various parts of the country for paltry sums, even by their parents, finding themselves unable to maintain their children on account of acute poverty and unbearable miseries and hoping that their children would be engaged only in household duties or manual labour. But those who are acting as pimps or brokers in the 'flesh trade', and brothel keepers who hunt for these teenage children and young girls to make money, either purchase or kidnap them by deceitful means and unjustly and forcibly inveigle them into the 'flesh trade'. Once these unfortunate victims are taken to the dens of prostitutes and sold to brothel keepers, they are shockingly and brutally treated and confined in complete seclusion in a tiny claustrophobic room for several days without food, until they succumb to the vicious desires of the brothel keepers and enter into the unethical and squalid business of prostitution. These victims, though unwilling to lead this obnoxious way of life, have no other option except to surrender themselves, retreating into silence and submitting their bodies to all the dirty customers, including even sexagenarians with plastic smiles.

The petition was for an order directing the Central Bureau of Investigation to institute an inquiry into the flourishing flesh trade and prosecute those found to be responsible. Further, an order was sought requiring all the inmates of red light areas and those engaged in the flesh trade to be removed to protective homes in the various states and provided with proper medical aid, shelter, education and training. Finally, the court was asked to direct that the children of prostitutes, children found begging in the streets and girls pushed into the flesh trade should be removed to protective homes and rehabilitated.

However, the court observed that legislation aimed at curbing the practice of prostitution and providing for rehabilitation of victims of the flesh trade was not achieving the desired result. It opined that the malady was not only social but also socio-economic in nature and, therefore, preventative rather than punitive measures should be taken. Consequently, a roving inquiry by the Central Bureau of Investigation was neither practical nor desirable.

The court directed, instead, that state governments should act swiftly, in terms of existing laws, to eradicate child prostitution; to set up advisory committees to make recommendations on further measures to eradicate child prostitution and on the implementation of social welfare programmes to provide care and rehabilitation for, in particular, the young 'fallen victim'; and to provide an adequate number of rehabilitation homes staffed by qualified social workers, psychiatrists and doctors.

In addition, the court ordered the central government to set up its own advisory committee which, in addition to the tasks set for its state counterparts, would also make suggestions regarding amendments to existing laws or new laws. The court noted that the matter was of great importance, warranting a comprehensive and searching analysis and requiring a humanistic rather than a purely legalistic approach.

Thus, in essence, the Supreme Court has tried to deal with the problem of prostitution by ordering the administration to do its job properly. It has intervened in the manner of doing that job only in so far as it has required the establishment of committees to analyse and solve the problem.

Another area in which the Supreme Court has played an innovative role is the troubling area of sexual assault against women. The decision of *Delhi Domestic Working Women's Forum vs Union of India and Others* included a direction to the National Commission for Women, established in January 1992, to develop a compensation and rehabilitation scheme aimed at 'wiping away the tears' of the victims of sexual assault. This public interest litigation was set in motion after four women employed as domestic workers alleged that they had been sexually assaulted by seven army personnel while travelling from Ranchi to Delhi by train. While prosecution of the soldiers was taking place, the court considering *Delhi Domestic Working Women's Forum* issued a number of guidelines for the assistance of victims of rape, who suffer a great deal of trauma and often find the experience of giving evidence in court as much of an ordeal as the rape itself. The court directed as follows:

- Victims of rape should be provided with legal representation.
- Legal representation should be provided at the police station itself, as these women arrive in a very distressed state.
- The police must inform the victim of her right to representation before asking her any questions.
- A list of advocates willing to act in such cases should be kept at police stations.
- To ensure that there is no delay, an advocate should be authorized to act even before leave of the court has been sought or obtained for the appointment.
- Anonymity of the victim should be maintained in rape trials.
- Having regard to the Directive Principles contained in Article 38(1), a Criminal Injury Compensation Board should be set up. Rape victims frequently incur financial loss as some are too traumatized to continue in employment.
- Compensation for victims should be awarded by the court on conviction of the offender, and by the Criminal Injuries Compensation Board whether or not the conviction has taken place. The board should take into account pain, suffering and shock, as well as loss of earnings due to pregnancy and the expenses of childbirth if this occurred as a result of the rape.

It is clear from the cases discussed above that the

Supreme Court has embraced an activist role in order to give relief to oppressed women. In relation to rape, it has called for a scheme to assist the rehabilitation of victims and for the establishment of a compensation board to provide victims with monetary relief. It has also insisted on the right of victims to legal aid and stated that this should be promptly provided.

With regard to the problems of prostitution, it has directed that committees at both state and national level should undertake in-depth investigations and suggest solutions. Similarly, in relation to the evils of the dowry system, it has attempted to protect women by requiring investigations into dowry-linked deaths to be undertaken by senior police officers and by ordering the creation of special investigative units including female social workers. So also, in regard to protective homes for women, the court has been prepared to involve itself in a supervisory role to attempt to ensure minimum standards of living and of care.

Overall, the court has actively upheld the rights to liberty, legal representation, legal aid and a speedy trial, and the right to live with dignity. It has issued directions aimed at improving conditions for women in police lock-ups and jails and made an effort to sensitize the police. It has prodded a sluggish administration into doing its duty in terms of implementation of laws. In short, the Supreme Court has taken the suffering of the poor and disadvantaged, including women, seriously and tried to help.

Social Action Litigation

Social action litigation in India is more than three decades old. It has taken root and the sapling has become a tree. Many more judges have become committed to this manner of litigation as a means to ensure social justice, which is a major theme of the Indian Constitution. Former critics who warned that social action litigation was an 'unruly horse' that could not be controlled and would cause the over-burdening of an already clogged court are having second thoughts. For they have seen, in the words of Lord Denning, that with a good person in the saddle, 'the unruly horse can be kept in control. It can jump over obstacles. It can leap fences put up by fictions and come down on the side of justice.'

But this does not mean that there were and are no difficulties. The question of locus standi (i.e., whether or not someone has the right to petition a court about a grievance), for example, took up a great deal of the court's time in the earlier cases, until its scope was enlarged.

In response to several questions in relation to the epistolary jurisdiction (i.e. treating a letter as a writ petition) and the validity of public interest litigation as a viable and judicially sound and acceptable mode of dispensing justice, the Supreme Court has established a procedure. The earlier practice where letters seeking judicial intervention were addressed to a particular judge, who then took up the matter, has been changed. The procedure requires the registration and listing of such cases according to certain guidelines. Slowly but surely, social action litigation has found both its procedure and its personnel. More lawyers are taking up social problems and filing proper writ petitions both in the High Courts and in the Supreme Court.

A problem that has been causing some anxiety is the question of the enforceability of the directives and orders of the court in relation to social action litigation. The Supreme Court has said it will take a serious view of failure to enforce its decisions but it has been reluctant to use the contempt procedure against non-compliant members of the executive or the administration. Since the relief is normally of a corrective nature, requiring a plan for the future and positive action from the administration, the court has tended to attempt to negotiate or partially negotiate the remedy. It has sought the assistance of panels of experts, commissions and advisory committees in framing schemes and/or laws to assist in the implementation of the rehabilitative process, and has tried to carry the administration along with it in the project of safeguarding the lives and dignity of the poor and downtrodden.

In relation to the status and rights of women, it is worth mentioning two important amendments to the Indian Constitution. These amendments require that one-third of the seats in both rural and urban local government bodies are occupied by women, and that one-third of the chairpersons of these institutions are women. These amendments have assisted in the empowerment of women at the local level, ensuring their participation in political decision making and helping them in their march towards social justice.

In this regard, a writ petition filed in the Madras High Court is of interest for the light it may shed on the effects changing social mores can have on the need for particular rights. The petition challenged Section 66 of the Factories Act of 1948, which was intended to protect women from exploitation and provided that they shall not be required or allowed to work in any factory at night. The petition arose from the desire of Soundararaja Mills to employ only women in a new factory manufacturing synthetic yarn for export, on the grounds that women are more efficient and hardworking. The women so employed were willing to work at night in order to meet the export delivery schedule. However, the law prevented them from doing so. Therefore, some women's groups, keen to see the gender-based differentiation of Section 66 removed, argued that the situation today is very different from that in 1948 when the law was enacted.

This serves to illustrate why public interest litigation has been referred to as initiatory democracy: it enables the person in the street to initiate actions aimed at giving effect to constitutional and legal principles that might otherwise remain remote ideas, or moderating legal provisions no longer adequate to their original intention. As the discussion in this essay has attempted to show, such initiatory democracy has enjoyed a great deal of support from the Indian courts. Indeed, there has been a striking departure in India from the fetters of Anglo-Saxon jurisprudence: when the judicial conscience has been shocked, procedural shackles have been shattered. Social action litigation has opened the doors of justice to all in India, establishing a body of precedent that should be useful to other developing countries which value the spirit as well as the letter of the rule of law.

Women's Rights

We all know that women are half the world and hold up half the sky. But where are they when it comes to equality?

Women represent 70 per cent of the poor according to a 2008 UN Report. Women are the majority of the world's illiterate. Worldwide, women earn less than men for doing equal work; the average gap in 2008 was 17 per cent. Their unpaid housework and family labour, if counted as a productive output in a national account, would increase measures of global output greatly. According to the 2008 UN report, if women's paid employment rates were raised to the same level as men's, 'America's GDP would be 9 per cent higher; the eurozone would be 13 per cent higher, and Japan's would be boosted by 16 per cent'. The concept of equality requires a level playing field. Treating persons who are in an unequal situation equally does not do away with the injustice. This situational imbalance has to be rectified first.

Though the United Nations made a beginning for the advancement of women with the signing of its founding charter, it was not until much later that anything effective was achieved. Only four women signed the UN Charter, and none of them headed a delegation. The members declared their faith 'in fundamental human rights, in the dignity and worth of the human person, in the equal rights of men and women and of nations large and small'.

In 1946 the Commission on the Status of Women was established and it has acted as a catalyst for much of what has been achieved by and for women over these last nearly seventy years. The landmark Convention on the Elimination of All Forms of Discrimination against Women (CEDAW) of 1979, often referred to as the Women's International Bill of Rights, is a dynamic document. As the name implies, it prohibits all forms of discrimination against women. It not only demands that women be given equal rights with men but also mentions the measures to be taken so that women can enjoy the rights to which they are entitled. Though the Universal Declaration of Human Rights of 1948 had referred to the equal rights of men and women and the dignity of the human person, it was felt that the 1979 Convention was necessary because despite the existence of this Declaration and the International Covenant on Economic, Social and Cultural Rights, 1966, the International Covenant on Civil and Political Rights, 1966 and its two optional Protocols, women still did not enjoy equal rights, and discrimination continued to exist in every society. The 1979 Convention identified many specific areas where there had been great discrimination: political rights, marriage and the family, and employment.

The convention was adopted by the General Assembly in 1979. It came into force after the necessary ratification in 1981 and thereafter the monitoring Committee on the Elimination of Discrimination against Women was formally established. It consists of twenty-three independent experts nominated by state parties. The committee has, since its inception, been composed mainly of women. It acts as a monitoring system to oversee the implementation of the convention by those states which have ratified it or acceded to it. This is done by examining the reports submitted by the state parties. It can also receive reports from non-governmental organizations and United Nations specialized agencies. As of 1 January 2008, the responsibility for servicing the committee has been transferred to the office of the High Commissioner for Human Rights in Geneva.

Before any binding international conventions or treaties came into existence, it was a matter of domestic jurisdiction as to how citizens were treated. It is only in the last sixty-five years that the international human rights system has started to function. Today the Commission on Human Rights is a body of state members, and its sub-commission is a body of experts that is concerned with human rights. But the truly remarkable institutional development in human rights has been the evolution of an international multilateral treaty regime with monitoring bodies. When the World Conference on Human Rights was held in Vienna in 1993, there were a number of important treaties in existence including the Convention on the Elimination of All Forms of Discrimination against Women and the Convention on the Rights of the Child. All states are free to join these treaties.

Apart from the most important monitoring mechanism, i.e. the examination of reports submitted by state parties, there are also regional mechanisms such as the European Convention on Human Rights and its Commission and Court, the Inter-American Convention with its Commission and Court and the African Charter on Human Rights and its Commission. These regional instruments and institutional arrangements appear to be stronger and 'more legally compelling' upon the state. A profound cultural change has come over the world in the last sixty-five years and has encouraged human rights to be regarded as an international concern. But as Dame Rosalyn Higgins (former president of the International Court of Justice) says: 'The institutional system—like international aviation—is at once wonderful and miraculous and on the very edge of chaos the entire time.'

International human rights law has not been applied effectively to address the disadvantages and injustices experienced by women, and this is primarily because they are women. As stated by Rebecca J. Cook (Human Rights professor, University of Toronto), the reasons for this general failure are complex and vary from country to country. They include lack of understanding of the systemic nature of the subordination of women. In the past there has been an unwillingness by traditional human rights groups to focus on violations of women's rights and a lack of understanding by women's groups of the potential use of international human rights law to vindicate women's rights.

For human rights to be effective, they have to become a part of the culture and tradition of a society. The institution of law in South Asia is generally viewed with deep suspicion and often hatred because it is often seen as the central instrument employed by colonizing powers to replace indigenous cultural, religious and social traditions with a mechanism of the modern Western nation states.

In some regions of the world, like India, mutual relations in all matters regarding marriage, divorce, maintenance, child custody, guardianship and inheritance are governed by personal law based on one's religious identity. This undermines the universality of the international prohibition of discrimination against women. Personal law that discriminates against women is often retained in India for reasons of political expediency. Let me give some examples of this discrimination.

A pertinent case is that of *Mohammed Ahmed Khan vs Shah Bano Begum and Others*. After more than forty years of marriage, Shah Bano's husband, an advocate, drove her out of their matrimonial home in 1975. For a short period he paid her a small maintenance. In April 1978, Shah Bano filed a petition for maintenance of ₹500 per month under Section 125 of the Criminal Procedure Code, which provided for prevention of destitution. While her application was pending, her husband unilaterally divorced her by pronouncing 'talaq' and paid the mahr (a sum agreed upon at the time of marriage) of ₹3,000. Thereafter, he refused to pay maintenance. The magistrate ordered him to pay the princely sum of ₹25 per month and the High Court raised the payment to ₹179.20. The husband appealed to the Supreme Court.

He stated that since he was a Muslim, his marriage was governed by Muslim Personal Law and that under that law there was no duty to pay maintenance, but only the duty of paying her the mahr. He submitted that personal law was superior to the Criminal Procedure Code. In 1985, the Supreme Court dismissed the husband's appeal, stating that the provisions of the Criminal Procedure Code for prevention of destitution did not conflict with Muslim law and rules of maintenance. It also noticed certain provisions of the Quran and stated that it imposed certain obligations on a Muslim husband to make provision for or to provide maintenance to his divorced wife.

The court observed that it was a matter of regret that Article 44 of the Constitution of India had remained a dead letter. This article provides that the state shall endeavour to secure for the citizens a Uniform Civil Code throughout India. But there had, so far, been no evidence of any official activity for framing such a code. The court appreciated the difficulties involved in bringing persons of different faiths and persuasions on a common platform, yet felt that the state had to make a beginning if the Constitution were to have any meaning. As the court said: 'Justice to all is a far more satisfactory way of dispensing justice than justice from case to case.'

The judgment was vehemently criticized by some Muslims and described as an interference in their personal law. Some members of the community raised a huge hue and cry and said that Islam itself was in danger! Muslim fundamentalists and religious leaders organized signature campaigns and demanded that the government introduce a bill exempting Muslim women from Section 125 of the Criminal Procedure Code. Women's groups and liberal organizations, on the other hand, carried out a country-wide campaign supporting the judgment on Shah Bano and the move for a Uniform Civil Code.

The government, though it had initially supported the Shah Bano judgment, got cold feet and completely changed its tune because of the political pressure that the Muslim groups brought to bear. It felt that it could not afford to alienate the Muslim fundamentalists, whom they saw as the key to an indispensable vote bank. So instead of having the political courage to move for a Uniform Civil Code, it took a step backward and introduced the Muslim Women (Protection of Rights on Divorce) Act, 1986 whereby Muslim women were taken out of the purview of Section 125 of the Criminal Procedure Code.

Who then would provide for a destitute Muslim wife? The new Act said that the Waqf Board would do so, even though it is well known that the Waqf Board is a body with meagre funds. Thus personal law was made superior to a provision in the Criminal Procedure Code. As a result, Shah Bano had no rights. She suffered as a woman, as a Muslim, and as a Muslim woman trying to assert a different voice within her community.

Without equity in the family, there cannot be equity in society. This action of the state of taking divorced, destitute Muslim women out of the purview of the prescribed law is violative of its obligation under CEDAW. It deprived Muslim women of a pre-existing right. The Government of India's decision of non-interference in the personal affairs of any community is in direct conflict with the purpose and object of the women's convention to improve the status of women. The state cannot justify inaction regarding women's rights on this basis. It cannot wait for the Muslim community to take the lead in the matter. It is bound by the Constitution of India and should not be influenced by the obscurantist views of religious leaders and others primarily concerned with preserving their patriarchy. It is a fraud on the women of India.

Another case of a fundamentalist nature is that of Roop Kanwar. In September 1987, Roop Kanwar, a Hindu, was burnt alive on her husband's funeral pyre. She was an 18-year-old university student living in Deorala, Rajasthan. The site of her cremation was considered a shrine and became a place of pilgrimage. Many people thought she was a goddess and that visiting her shrine would cure them of cancer—the illness that took the life of her husband.

There are many versions that explain how she committed sati. According to some, she was willing to die, and according to others she was coerced into it, or was hesitant and succumbed to family pressure. The local people claimed that the right to commit sati was part of their ethnic culture. Women's groups throughout India were horrified and organized a march in Rajasthan. And the debate raged: Was sati right if it was voluntary and a time-honoured practice in Rajasthan? It was said that it would be cultural discrimination to prevent someone who wished to commit sati from doing so. They said that the practice, if it is to be done away with, must be eliminated by the people and the community of Rajasthan and not by the central government. But women felt that sati was so offensive that the onus, as in custodial rape, should shift to the family to prove that coercion had not taken place. The government was in a dilemma. People in Rajasthan, after all, were celebrating the event as a courageous act.

After months of delay, the police finally arrested Roop Kanwar's father-in-law and five other members of the family for abetment to suicide. A few months later, Parliament passed a law banning sati even though an older law already existed. This was to show that this ethnic practice was utterly reprehensible and barbaric. Many Hindi language newspapers, however, stated that human rights consciousness was a product of the urban Western intelligentsia and that the human rights people were out to denigrate national culture.

What is the use of all the laws and international conventions and covenants if the local people are not convinced that putting a young woman on the funeral pyre of her husband and burning her to death is wrong?

One ray of hope is that the practice has now been

more or less obliterated except for the rare exception, while a hundred years ago about 600 women committed sati every year. In those days, when sati took place, there was no expression of outrage from women. It was an accepted custom for a young widow to immolate herself on her husband's funeral pyre. The change of attitude was brought about by social reformers such as Raja Ram Mohan Roy and others who campaigned vigorously for widow remarriage.

A third very interesting case which brings out many aspects of human rights violation is that of the social worker Bhanwari Devi, who carried out a vigorous campaign against child marriage. (This case has been discussed in detail in the essay 'Gender Sensitization of the Judiciary'.) When she succeeded in preventing the marriage of a one-year-old girl, she was allegedly gang-raped. At the trial, it was alleged not only that Bhanwari Devi was raped in order to satiate the lust of a few men, but also that humiliation was inflicted upon her because of her campaign against child marriage, which went against the feudal set-up. But the District and Sessions judge, Jaipur, acquitted the accused on the grounds that they were middle-aged men of good social status and well placed in the caste hierarchy and therefore incapable of wishing to rape a lower caste woman.

I am told that after the rape it had been suggested to Bhanwari Devi that she leave the village. However, she said, 'I have not done anything wrong and I will continue to stay in Bhateri.' She was socially boycotted and her community ostracized her; her in-laws and neighbours despised her and called her a shame to the village as if it were she who had committed a crime. A lesser woman would have given up but she fought it out. During her in camera trial, she had to testify in front of seventeen men. It was virtually a re-enactment of the rape. She went through hell and even after the unjust judgment she was not ready to give up. She said, 'I will continue my fight till I get justice... How can I ask people to fight for justice when I am unable to get justice from the state even though I am a government servant?'

And while justice has eluded Bhanwari Devi, her courage has not been in vain. Following this case, the Vishakha Guidelines came into effect (through a public interest litigation filed in the Supreme Court) and more recently the Sexual Harassment of Women at Workplace (Prevention, Prohibition and Redressal) Act, 2013 was also passed; this, as its title implies, seeks to protect women from sexual harassment at the workplace and creates a mechanism for the redressal of complaints.

■

The Constitution of India not only grants equality to women but also empowers the state to adopt measures of affirmative discrimination in favour of women. The Constitution further imposes a duty on every citizen to renounce practices derogatory to the dignity of women. But even today, most women in India have neither the freedom nor the liberty to take decisions. Though they hold up half the sky, their voice is muted. Often they are not even allowed to decide whether they can have a child and, if they have a girl child, whether they can keep her. Injustice such as this cannot be allowed to continue.

A Uniform Civil Code towards Gender Justice

Over sixty-four years ago we, the people of India, gave ourselves a wonderful Constitution—envisioning a sovereign, democratic republic where there would be justice, liberty, equality and fraternity. The Constitution secured for us certain fundamental rights, and the right to enforce them through the courts. Other aspirations, which could not be achieved immediately, were placed in the next chapter, titled Directive Principles of State Policy. These were directions to the Indian state for implementation in due course, except where there was a time frame mentioned, such as ten years in the case of providing free and compulsory education for all children till the age of 14 years. Unfortunately, even this time frame was not adhered to, leading the Supreme Court in 1993 to treat it as a right and to demand compliance. This eventually resulted in a constitutional amendment in 2002 and ultimately in the Right of Children to Free and Compulsory Education Act, 2009 (RTE Act, 2009), which came into force on 1 April 2010.

Article 44 of the Constitution provides for a Uniform

Civil Code for the citizens of the country. It states: 'The State shall endeavour to secure for the citizens a Uniform Civil Code throughout the territory of India.' What does Uniform Civil Code mean here? We already had a uniform criminal code—one that applied to all in the territory of India. We also had a number of civil laws which were uniform—like the Contract Act, Transfer of Property Act and the Civil Procedure Code. So, this Uniform Civil Code really referred to family laws, sometimes called personal laws.

The Muslim members of the constituent assembly who voiced their opinion on the Uniform Civil Code were all men. Except for Tajamul Hussain from Bihar, all of them fought relentlessly to exclude this provision. At the other end of the spectrum were three stalwarts for social change and equality for women—Minoo Masani, a Parsi; Rajkumari Amrit Kaur, a Christian; and Hansa Mehta, a Hindu—who wanted it to be made a fundamental right.

Neither viewpoint was accepted and it was made a Directive Principle of State Policy—postponing the problem to be sorted out by a future government. And that's where the issue has remained.

Successive governments have not shown the necessary gumption and courage to act upon it. Though off and on the need for a Uniform Civil Code is debated, a small but vociferous section of the Muslim community—India's largest minority—opposes it on grounds of religious interference; and the larger but quieter voice of gender justice is dispelled, resulting in uncertainties and continued discrimination. It is in this context that one should remember the words of Acharya Kripalani, a Congressman, when the Hindu personal laws were being radically reformed in 1955–1956 despite the vociferous opposition of an orthodox president and many Hindu religious leaders. He said:

> We call our State a secular State—A secular State goes neither by scripture nor by custom. It must work on sociological and political grounds. If we are a democratic State, I submit we must make laws not for one community alone. Today the Hindu community is not as much prepared for divorce as the Muslim community is for monogamy... Will our government introduce a Bill for monogamy for the Muslim community? Will my dear Law Minister apply the part about monogamy to every community in India?... I tell you this is the democratic way. It is not the Mahasabhaites alone who are communal; it is the government also that is communal, whatever it may say. It is passing a communal measure. You shall be known by your acts, not by your profession. You have deluded the world so often with words. I charge you with communalism because you are bringing forward a law about monogamy only for the Hindu community.
>
> You must bring it also for the Muslim community... the Muslim community is prepared to have it but you are not brave enough to do it.

The government was silent and went ahead as planned.

The government is still silent, decades later. A courageous government could have ensured equality and justice for all Indian women then; a progressive government should ensure equality and justice for all Indian women now by pushing through a Uniform Civil Code.

■

Though the Constitution does say that Directive Principles are not enforceable by any court, it also makes it clear that the Directive Principles are 'fundamental in the governance of the country and it shall be the duty of the State to apply these principles in making laws'.

Article 44 pertains to all citizens of India. The Constitution confers citizenship not on the basis of caste, creed, sex or religion, but on the basis of birth, domicile, choice, etc. It is the right of all citizens, and women in particular, to be treated equally and without being discriminated against, and the endeavour of the state to achieve this must be perpetual and paramount. Even if the government hesitates for fear of losing votes and religious leaders rant for fear of losing power, the women's movement and civil society should not be discouraged. They must help bring about equality for all Indian women, including those whose voices haven't been heard because they have been in purdah for years. We cannot leave it only to the minority community to raise the issue, for then we might wait forever, since it does not suit most men to give up their hold on women or any advantage that is already theirs.

This was brought home to me very clearly at a seminar I attended in Lahore in August 1995, organized by the Legal Aid Cell of AGHS on Family Laws and Human Rights of Women. It dealt with the personal laws in Bangladesh, India and Pakistan.

It was apparent that though the family laws for the Muslim majorities in Pakistan and Bangladesh had changed somewhat since Partition and benefited women in those countries, the position of the Hindu minority remained as it was before. The substantial benefits gained by Hindu women in India on issues like mandatory monogamy, permitting divorce, the right of women to adopt and inheritance rights, etc. had passed them by, and they were still carrying on as before. Similarly, while some benefits had accrued in Bangladesh and Pakistan to Muslim women by virtue of Muslim Personal Law amendments brought about in those two countries, the Muslim minority in India had been passed over without any movement towards gender-just laws.

Since changing laws for minorities is a sensitive matter, at this seminar we called upon 'concerned persons, social action groups, political parties, legislators, and the governments of these countries to campaign for and introduce reforms in the family laws in order to make them just and guarantee equal rights to all women and children'.

A declaration setting out 'the minimum requirements' was released. It dealt with marriage, separation and divorce as well as guardianship, custody, adoption, and other rights of the child; and it made provisions regarding economic rights of women within marriage, and with regard to maintenance and inheritance laws.

These are not demands for Hindu or Muslim or Christian or Parsi laws; these are a cry for gender-just laws, for giving all women their human rights and their mandated constitutional rights. If we cannot guarantee them all the rights in one go, let us at least progress slowly and incrementally rather than remaining stagnant.

I say that we must depoliticize the question of the Uniform Civil Code. For at the heart of the desire for a Uniform Civil Code is the determination to do away with discrimination; to empower women, and to give them their dignity and self-esteem. A Uniform Civil Code (in other words, a uniform family law code) will help break down customary practices derogatory and harmful to women and give women their individual identity as independent citizens of India.

Religion is about faith—a relationship between an individual and his god—whereas law is about specific rights of an individual as against other individuals or society at large. I strongly disagree with commentators such as Mani Shankar Aiyar who says (in *Confessions of a Secular Fundamentalist*): 'As the customs and usages, rites and rituals, traditions and practices of different communities are the very basis on which religious communities distinguish themselves from each other, the prospect of actually securing a Uniform Civil Code is distant.'

Law and religion are separate. There can be one law for all Indians even if many religions are practised and diverse customs followed. Although Jains, Buddhists and Sikhs fall within the ambit of Hindu law, they follow their own religions and rituals.

There is the religious plane, which is entirely personal and there is the social plane, which deals with a person's status and self-esteem as a citizen of the country. Take for instance the Divorce Act which applies to Christians, irrespective of whether they are Protestants or Catholics. The Catholic Church does not recognize divorce, but a Catholic can get a divorce under the provisions of this Act if he or she wants.

If criminal law treats all offenders with an equal hand—regardless of their caste, creed, sex and religion—so should civil law, including family law. Women's lives are almost invariably bound up with the family and their status therein. Laws that are unjust within the family or larger society cannot stand within the framework of the Constitution and must slowly but surely be changed.

■

I was a member of the 15th Law Commission of India (1997-2000). We submitted a number of reports to the government. When I suggested to Justice Jeevan Reddy, the chairperson of the 15th Law Commission of India, that we take up the question of the Uniform Civil Code and write a report on it, he looked thoughtful and said, 'This is not the right time.' And indeed, the timing—which of course will never be perfect—is a vexed question. It is difficult to get minority communities to accept such legislation if they are suspicious of the partisan motives of the government that seeks to introduce it.

Our report on the Indian Divorce Act, 1869, took us into the realm of personal law. The Divorce Act applied only to Christians, and was heavily weighted against women. Despite several reports—one as early as 1960—by previous law commissions, the law had not been changed. Once again we made suggestions in the context of the notorious Section 10 of the Act, which provided that a Christian man could be granted divorce on the ground of adultery alone, whereas a Christian woman had to establish adultery plus an additional matrimonial offence such as cruelty or bigamy or incest or desertion. This was obviously discriminatory and we wanted it changed.

We recommended that the anomalies and ambiguities be removed and the law be changed expeditiously in the interest of social justice. The new law came into force in September 2001.

The 15th Law Commission also took up the property rights of women in Hindu personal law. The Mitakshara system of the Hindu joint family (commonly known as the Hindu undivided family or HUF), where devolution of property takes place by survivorship rather than succession, permits only sons to be members of the coparcenary. We felt that the exclusion of daughters from participating in coparcenary property, merely by reason of their sex, was unjust, and we made some positive recommendations in this context.

Kerala had abolished the legal entity of the Hindu joint family in 1975; Andhra Pradesh, through a 1986 Act, mandated that daughters too would become coparceners; Tamil Nadu (1989), Maharashtra (1994) and Karnataka (1994) followed the Andhra Pradesh model. After deliberation, we decided to recommend a combination of the two models. That is, daughters would first be made coparceners like sons so that they would be entitled to get their share on partition or on the death of the male coparcener; these shares would then be held by everyone as 'tenants in common'. We believed that the synthesis we arrived at was in keeping with justice, equity and family harmony. We suggested that these changes be brought about by an amendment to the central act by Parliament so that there would be uniformity across the country.

In May 2000, our report, 'Property Rights of Women: Proposed Reforms under the Hindu Law', was sent to the union law minister. This was the last report submitted by the 15th Law Commission, whose term was to expire at the end of August. The press reported it extensively.

When some TV reporters came to the Law Commission to interview me on the subject, I said:

> Despite the Constitution of India having proclaimed equality before the law as a fundamental right, a daughter is excluded from participation in ancestral property under the Mitakshara system merely by reason

of her sex. It is my fervent hope that if the changes suggested are brought about and fully implemented it will be the death knell for the curse of dowry and will also improve the condition of women.

Discrimination against women enshrined in the law exists just as acutely in the Muslim Personal Law in India. What is worse is that here, attempts by the courts to improve their position have roused the wrath of sections of the community. In the Shah Bano case, an impoverished divorced woman denied maintenance by her ex-husband was granted it by the Supreme Court on grounds other than those of Muslim Personal Law.

It is worth pointing out that in the latter case, the subsequent uproar compelled the pusillanimous, vote-seeking government of the day to rush a bill, the speciously titled 'Muslim Women (Protection of Rights on Divorce) Bill' through Parliament in order to nullify the Supreme Court judgment and deny Muslim women this protection. It was a shameful capitulation. (This has been dealt with in more detail in the essay 'Women's Rights'.)

■

In December 2004 the then law minister presented to the cabinet a proposal to amend the Hindu Succession Act, 1956. He mentioned that the Law Commission had proposed reforms under the Hindu law in order to invest women with equal coparcenary rights. And indeed, subsequently, the daughter has been made a coparcener by birth in the joint property through the Hindu Succession (Amendment) Act, 2005. However, when questioned by some of his colleagues, including the distinguished lawyer Fali Nariman, about introducing a Uniform Civil Code, the law minister ruled it out, saying, 'We can't speak for all communities unless they are ready.'

But when will all communities be ready? Was the Hindu community ready when the shastric Hindu laws were drastically changed in 1955–1956? And how do we help the communities to be ready?

The answer appears to lie in the editorial of *The Hindu* (7 December 2004) which concluded that 'a readiness to reform can be created by dialogue and debate addressing the laws that discriminate against women grossly and are indefensible'.

It is important to bring all personal laws within the constitutional principle of equality. The Parsi, Christian and Hindu laws have been slowly moving in that direction, but we need the Muslim Personal Law to move likewise. After all, so many changes have been brought about in other countries where Muslims predominate. Why then should Indian Muslim women be so disadvantaged, especially when they have an equal right to vote and participate in the formation of government at both the state and central levels? Depriving them of equality in personal laws is both cruel and anomalous.

■

The line between personal law and criminal law is often

blurred. Section 125 of the Criminal Procedure Code is a provision to prevent vagrancy and thus give all Indian wives some maintenance. Yet it became a huge issue in the Shah Bano case. Again, when tribals marry, it is according to their personal law. If the panchayat shuns and shames them, it is seen to be following the law of the panchayat. But if the panchayat executes them, it is a case of murder and clearly a matter to be dealt with under criminal law. But is not blackening people's faces, putting garlands of shoes around their necks and ostracizing them also a violation of their human rights, and thus a crime?

Tribals suffer untold indignities, even death, for infringing tribal custom, yet leaders like the late Mahendra Singh Tikait proclaimed loudly that anyone breaking caste rules must expect to be punished. Muslim women suffer indignities as a result of horrendous practices, like divorce by triple talaq, etc., and though the All India Muslim Personal Law Board admits it is a social evil, the board president has said that the triple talaq is irrevocable as it comes from divine inspiration, namely the Shariat.

It is sometimes questioned why we need a Uniform Civil Code at all when we have the Special Marriage Act, 1954, which anyone, regardless of religion, may avail of and which Pandit Jawaharlal Nehru called the forerunner of the Uniform Civil Code. But the Special Marriage Act does not deal with personal laws, and parties marrying under this act are governed by the Indian Succession Act, 1925, and its subsequent amendments for purposes of inheritance.

Others suggest an optional code. But what use is that? There is no doubt that we live in a male-oriented society and only a few liberal and generous men will give up voluntarily what they have enjoyed over centuries. If in 1955–1956 we had enacted a voluntary Hindu code, how many Hindu men would have opted for it, especially as it was greatly at variance with existing Hindu religious laws? It is only because it was made mandatory that today Hindu women have benefited from it. We need to thank the champions of women's equality like Pandit Jawaharlal Nehru who had the courage and tact to see it through against all odds. He said he was happy that he could help his Hindu sisters, but regretted that he could not alter the law to benefit his Muslim sisters. The Supreme Court, in Shah Bano's case, and many other cases, also regretted that Article 44 has remained a dead letter.

In India, women's problems are similar, regardless of their caste, community, or religion. Women are suppressed and denied their dignity. A multiplicity of family laws divides and confuses them and they are often not aware of what their rights, if any, are in a given situation. They would feel strengthened if they were governed by one set of just rules. The larger group of uneducated women often cannot differentiate between custom, culture, religion and criminal law. Why should the Muslim Aneesa be at a disadvantage to the Hindu Parvati? Dr Vasudha Dhagamwar noticed in her research that Aneesa Begum, who worked as a domestic servant, was not willing to accept that if her husband Sayeed divorced her, she would not be entitled to maintenance like Parvati, a Hindu servant and similarly placed. She said: 'How won't they give it? Parvati will get it and I won't? How can this be? Is there no law in the country?' Her exact words were 'Desh mein koi kanoon hai ya nahin?' Just as with criminal law, family or personal law should also be the same for all individuals, so that a plethora of personal laws does not prevent some women from having rights of equality available to others. A uniform family law prevails in most countries. Indeed, it prevails even in Goa, where it is a legacy of Portuguese rule.

One of the advantages of a Uniform Civil Code would be a proper notice period for and registration of any marriage. While people can have religious ceremonies of their choice (or not have any ceremony at all), proof of the marriage would be the registration of and compliance with the procedure set out in the Uniform Civil Code. Monogamy would be mandatory and the laws of divorce would be the same for men and women. This will lead to a cohesive and non-fragmented society. Men and women must be entitled to equal property rights that can be enforced by law. This will constitute real empowerment for women.

But bringing in such a Uniform Civil Code will not be easy, as we have seen. Witness the government's attempt, in 1972, to bring in a comprehensive all-India law on adoption, aiming to supersede the existing Hindu law on adoption. The bill went to the select committee and it was opposed, even though it was only an enabling act, not a compulsory one. A completely secular law was lost because one community opposed it on religious grounds, claiming that Islam doesn't permit adoption, though a 'bad' Muslim might adopt. A Muslim member of the community even went so far as to say that there should be no such law giving any community 'the liberty of abandoning their personal law'.

Earlier still, Dr Ambedkar could not persuade the government to get the Hindu Code Bill passed in one go, in spite of the fact that it was built on gender justice. It had to be split up and passed piecemeal during the period 1955–1956: marriage in 1955, and succession, minority and guardianship, and adoption and maintenance staggered over 1956. For reasons of political expediency just family laws were not enacted for all Indian women. Thus only Hindu women benefited—as well as Sikh, Buddhist and Jain women, who were included in these laws.

It is no use closing the debate and saying, as Mani Shankar Aiyar says in his book, that there is one and only one factor standing in the way of the reform of Muslim personal law—the demand for 'immediate imposition by brute majority of a Uniform Civil Code on the Muslims by a political party' which is communalist and anti-Muslim and which in the guise of a Uniform Civil Code wishes to impose a Hindu civil code. What Mr Aiyar fails to note is that Indian women are not asking for a Hindu civil code but a Uniform Civil Code, one that is most just and fair to women.

Why should a decades-old demand and commitment

made in the Constitution be abandoned? What I say is do not oppose it because a particular party supports it—depoliticize it and remember that a good idea propounded by the Constitution does not become bad because your opponents tried to hijack it. Jointly ensure that it is gender-just, and get the credit for women's emancipation and equality. Take what is best in all laws and frame a Uniform Civil Code.

We have a duty to the women of India to do away with all discrimination between men and women and make a personal law that will benefit all Indian women without distinction, be they Christian, Hindu, Muslim, Parsi, Sikh or Buddhist. Law is a springboard and a 'pointer', in the words of Gandhiji, and itself helps to bring about the change in mindset required for effective implementation. American theologian and ethicist Reinhold Niebuhr said: 'Man's capacity for justice makes democracy possible, but man's inclination to injustice makes democracy necessary.' Let us do things in a democratic manner and give justice to women.

I speak not as a Hindu or an agnostic but as a woman who feels the indignity suffered by other women, and as a secularist (though not a 'secular fundamentalist', a term which has acquired a pejorative meaning). Change requires hard work. It needs dialogue and public debate and convincing people with empathy. It is no use taking purely adversarial positions. That will not get women anywhere. Let us prepare a good draft and circulate it widely. Let us also circulate the family law bills prepared by the National Commission for Women and others. It is important for the matter to be discussed in a transparent manner so that ignorance, which is the cradle of prejudice and fear, is removed. The process must be open. We must not let the fundamentalists—Hindu, Muslim, Christian or secular—take over. We should bring the light of reason and humanity to bear on the subject and act tactfully but bravely. So let us slowly move into the sunlight for, in the words of Martin Luther King, 'Injustice anywhere is a threat to justice everywhere'.

Children's Rights

The welfare and rights of the child have evoked universal concern for some time past. Since the days of the League of Nations, commitments for the protection of children have been scattered through various international treaties and declarations. The Geneva Declaration, containing five principles, was adopted on 26 September 1924. It stated that necessary means must be given for the physical and spiritual development of the child, and specifically provided that a child must be educated and protected against exploitation. Thereafter, the landmark 1948 Universal Declaration of Human Rights proclaimed that children as a category are entitled to special care and assistance. Article 26 recognizes the right to compulsory free education, at least in the elementary and fundamental stages.

On 20 November 1959, the Declaration of the Rights of the Child was proclaimed by the General Assembly of the United Nations. It contained ten principles which enriched and developed the 1924 Geneva Declaration. Exactly thirty years later, on 20 November 1989, the General Assembly unanimously adopted the Convention on the Rights of the Child. It entered into force on 2 September 1990, having been ratified by the required twenty states. The convention has been spoken of as the most complete statement of children's rights with the force of international law.

The earlier UN Declaration of the Rights of the Child in 1959, though an international instrument, carried no binding legal obligation, whereas the convention demands an active decision on the part of the individual states ratifying it. Further, a mechanism for monitoring compliance is an integral function of the convention and the signatory states are obliged to report to a Committee on the Rights of the Child. Though, admittedly, there is no provision for either inter-state or individual complaints, the fact that the ratifying states agree to submit regular reports (which are made public) to the committee provides an element of quasi-legal accountability.

The convention recognizes the special vulnerability of children and deals not only with civil and political rights but also economic, social, cultural and humanitarian rights, which are interdependent. It has a holistic approach and acknowledges that although a child may be adequately nourished, its right to develop fully is not properly protected unless it is also educated and shielded from such things as arbitrary detention and exploitation at work. The main underlying principle of the convention is that the best interests of the child shall always be the major consideration and that the child's own opinion shall be given due regard. The child is recognized as an individual with needs which evolve with age and maturity. Consequently, the child has been given the right to participate in decisions affecting its present and future, and a child's rights are balanced with the rights and duties of parents or others who are responsible for its survival, development and protection.

The preamble to the convention recalls the basic principles of the United Nations and specific provisions of certain relevant human rights treaties and proclamations. It reaffirms the fact that children, because of their vulnerability, need special care and protection; and it places special emphasis on the primary care and protective responsibility of the family, the need for legal and other protection of the child before and after birth, the importance of respect for the cultural values of the child's community, and the vital role of international cooperation in achieving the realization of children's rights.

The convention's fifty-four articles are divided into three parts: Part I (Articles 1 to 41) deals with the various rights; Part II (Articles 42 to 45) provides for dissemination of information and the appointment of a committee for examining the progress made by the state parties in achieving the obligations undertaken in the convention; and Part III (Articles 46 to 54) deals with ratification, accession and amendment. The rights contained in Part I pertain to such diverse subjects as name, nationality, non-discrimination, adoption, exploitation, education, health, liberty, leisure, labour and participation. It defines the child as a person under 18 unless, by national law, majority is attained at an earlier age.

The convention also deals with the problems of refugee children, sexual and other forms of child exploitation, drug abuse, children in trouble with the law, inter-country adoption, children in armed conflict, and the needs of disabled children and the children of minority or indigenous groups.

The coming into force of the convention is a positive step in reaching out to a better tomorrow. Though methods of upbringing and socialization can vary greatly from one country to another, there is no dispute that all communities and nations basically want the best for their children and have similar reactions if children are subjected to torture or deprivation, are maimed in armed conflict, or are separated from their families. As a result of this 'common denominator', the convention states that the child should be raised to its full potential under ideals proclaimed in the Charter of the United Nations, in the spirit of peace, dignity, tolerance, freedom, equality and solidarity. This provides the ratifying states with the motivation to make a positive effort for the harmonious and full development of the child, despite differing priorities from one country or situation to another.

The rights of the child are increasingly becoming an important consideration of international concern and action. The UN Convention on the Rights of the Child has now been ratified by all countries except Somalia and the United States. India ratified it in 1992. It is the most widely subscribed Human Rights Treaty.

The future of the world will depend on how it helps to shape the values of children and stimulate their aspirations. It has been said that the struggle to save children's lives must go hand in hand with an effort to change the lives thus saved; and that it is a cruel paradox that children whose lives are being saved are growing up in a world in which their prospects for self-betterment are actually diminishing. India and China together constitute one-third of the world's population and India has the largest number of uneducated children and working children. So it is crucially important to examine this aspect.

What does the 1990 UN Convention say about education and child labour and what is India's constitutional mandate?

Apart from other provisions, Articles 28 and 32 of the convention deal directly with these questions. Below are the relevant portions:

Article 28:
States Parties recognize the right of the child to education, and with a view to achieving this right progressively and on the basis of equal opportunity, they shall, in particular:
(a) Make primary education compulsory and available free to all...

Article 32:
1. States Parties recognize the right of the child to be protected from economic exploitation and from performing any work that is likely to be hazardous or to interfere with the child's education, or to be harmful

to the child's health or physical, mental, spiritual, moral or social development.
2. States Parties shall take legislative, administrative, social and educational measures to ensure the implementation of this article. To this end, and having regard to the relevant provisions of other international instruments, States Parties shall in particular:
   (a) Provide for a minimum age or minimum ages for admission to employment;
   (b) Provide for appropriate regulation of the hours and conditions of employment;
   (c) Provide for appropriate penalties or other sanctions to ensure the effective enforcement of the present article.

The important words in Article 32 in connection with the problem being discussed are that the child is to be protected from performing any work that will 'interfere with the child's education'.

That primary education for every child is the best investment that India can make has been recognized in our Constitution. Article 45 of the Indian Constitution provides for free and compulsory education within a time frame. It says: 'The State shall endeavour to provide, within a period of ten years from the commencement of this Constitution, for free and compulsory education for all children until they complete the age of fourteen years'.

Article 46 deals with the promotion of education and economic interests of scheduled castes, scheduled tribes and other weaker sections; and Article 41 with the right to work and education.

Article 24 as originally proposed by Dr K. M. Munshi prohibited child labour 'in all forms', but it was re-cast and re-formulated and reads: 'No child below the age of fourteen years shall be employed to work in any factory or mine or engaged in any hazardous employment'.

Article 39(e) speaks of 'the tender age of children not being abused' and 39(f) of them being given opportunities and facilities to develop in a free, healthy and dignified manner.

Though more than six decades have passed since 26 January 1950, when the Constitution came into force, the endeavour of the state has not become a reality. This is because, despite rhetoric and mantras, the state has not given universal primary education the priority and financial support it deserves and needs.

Myron Weiner, in his book *The Child and the State in India*, observed that, in India, education has been largely an instrument for differentiation by separating children according to social class. For this reason, those who control the education system are remarkably indifferent to the low enrolment and high dropout rate among the lowest social classes. The result is one of the highest rates of child labour in the world, one of the lowest rates of school attendance, and a literacy rate that has fallen behind most of the developing world. Further, the Indian government accepts child labour as a 'harsh reality' and proposes that measures be taken to improve working conditions for children rather than to remove them from the work force. The key notion in the child labour policy in India is 'amelioration' not 'abolition', and in education 'incentive' and not 'compulsion'. Many officials regard education for the masses not as liberating but as destabilizing. They question the value of compulsion. They say that the state has no right to force children to attend schools and thereby deny parents the benefit of their income. Some point out the economic benefits to the country of child labour, especially in export industries such as carpet weaving, where the manual dexterity of children and their low wages enhance the industry's capacity to compete in world markets.

It is true that many parents feel that it is better for their 10-year-old to learn to become a carpenter or carpet weaver or to graze cattle and look after the siblings rather than go to school; they think they have no choice and that they need the income and services of the child; and they do not appreciate the advantages gained from schooling. But what do the children themselves think?

A group of girls in a village near Pune, who had been enrolled and then taken out of school to look after their siblings, fetch water and firewood and care for the cattle, said they had left school at the request of their mothers. It was apparent that this was not what they wanted. When questioned further, the children said that they would ensure that their own daughters went to school and would, if necessary, send their babies to their mothers-in-law or a crèche, or arrange for someone else to watch over the smaller children. The cattle would be brought together and someone hired to look after them. Thus the children clearly did not regard their parents' decision about their schooling as the correct one, nor did they regard their parents as being without choice in the matter.

Parents must be made aware that investment in the child is more important than the additional income they can get from their children. This is poignantly brought home by the attitude of a particular official who was strongly opposed to child labour. He said:

> I belong to a scheduled caste community in the Punjab. We had no land, we were agricultural labourers. We had no money to spend on festivals. At nine my father took me out of school and sent me to work. I rebelled and wanted to stay in school. I even threatened suicide! So, my parents agreed to let me stay in school. I was at the top of my class, so I stayed on in school and went to college. Ultimately, I entered the Indian Administrative Service. I was the oldest child and other members of my family, my younger brothers and sisters, followed me to school. I don't think my father was so poor that he had to send me to work, but it was not the custom in his family to send children to school. Many parents do not think, but just send their children to work. If we in the Government emphasise that children should not be sent to work, they will go to school. Now all my children are in college. If I had listened

to my father I would still have been working in the village. (Weiner, 1991)

In India there does not appear to be a clear relationship between literacy and per capita income, in the sense of low income being the reason for not sending a child to school. For example, the state of Kerala, which has a very high literacy rate, has a per capita income that is basically no different from that of the rest of the country. Figures indicate that enrolment in schools has increased substantially in other states too. But statistics are very confusing since there is a great difference between mere initial enrolment and continuing in school for a number of years.

A study conducted at the Giri Institute of Social Sciences in Uttar Pradesh indicated that for every 100 children admitted into first grade, only thirty-five passed into fifth grade and only twenty completed eight years of schooling. The majority of dropouts were Muslims and Scheduled Castes; and girls had a particularly low enrolment and high dropout rate. Further, increase in rural income in western Uttar Pradesh as a result of the Green Revolution did not result in a rise in school enrolment or a decline in dropouts. A direct relationship between enrolment and the number of children in the family, especially in the case of girls, was noticed. For instance, if there were many young siblings, the older children stayed home to take care of younger ones. However, if there was one educated member in the family, then the children were more likely to be kept in school; and they stayed in school if the schools were attractive and had play facilities and programmes that held their interest.

Some people in India feel that we cannot afford to do without the labour of children as we are a poor country. Does that mean that the elimination of poverty is a pre-condition to prohibiting child labour? And does compulsory primary or universal elementary education have to wait till poverty is totally eliminated? The main argument against compulsory education is that child labour is necessary for the well-being of the poor, since the state is unable to provide relief. The second argument is that education would make the poor unsuited for the kind of manual work that is required to be done. The third argument is that certain industries would be forced to close down if they did not have access to low wage child labour. The last argument against banning child labour and enforcing compulsory education is that the state should not be allowed to interfere with parents' rights, since parents know what is best for their children and families. But the real question is: can we afford to have child labour and still talk of tomorrow's citizens? If ignorance grows, will the child of today have any choices tomorrow? Will he or she not feel trapped?

Take the case of the match factories in Sivakasi in Tamil Nadu, where labour conditions were horrendous and exploitation of child labour rampant. Even before the Child Labour (Prohibition and Regulation) Act, 1986 came into force, child labour was banned in the Sivakasi factories as it involved hazardous employment, but this simply pushed the children from the organized sector into the unorganized sector, where they were less visible. In *M.C. Mehta vs State of Tamil Nadu*, the Supreme Court held that though children cannot be employed within the match factories directly engaged in the manufacturing process, they can be employed in the process of packing, but it directed that this be done in an area away from the place of manufacture in order to avoid exposure to accidents.

India has a ₹2,600-crore carpet industry and a large number of children are employed in this industry as manufacturers believe that a child's nimble fingers are necessary for good weaving. But is the making and exporting of carpets more important than the education and welfare of the child? There is no doubt that children are a source of cheap labour and that this is the main reason for their employment in many industries. Of course, this also adds to adult unemployment. If primary education is effectively and compulsorily implemented and child labour withdrawn, will the entire Indian economy collapse? No. The industry will be forced to hire adults to make bangles, produce fireworks, matches, carpets, etc. A positive stand has to be taken, otherwise there will be only a process of continuation and drift.

In 1978 it was stated that in ten years child labour would be abolished. In 1988 this was stated once again. Twenty-five years on, this is still not the case. Social action is required to ensure that primary education takes place on a universal, compulsory basis. As far as our policies and promises are concerned, we adopted a National Policy for Children in 1974, a Statement of Health in 1983, a Policy of Education in 1986, and one on Child Labour in 1987. Operation Blackboard was launched in 1987, DIET (a nationwide scheme for District Institutes for Education and Training) and the Total Literacy Campaign in 1988, and a programme of Minimum Levels of Learning in 1989. A National Plan for Children was published in 1992. A National Commission for Protection of Child Rights was set up in 2007 under Commissions for Protection of Child Rights Act, 2005.

The 83rd Constitutional Amendment Bill making the right to primary education a fundamental right was introduced in Parliament in the Rajya Sabha on 28 July 1997. It was passed five years later, in 2002, as the 86th Constitutional Amendment Act, and Article 21A was thereby introduced into the Constitution.

It is only thereafter that the Right of Children to Free and Compulsory Education Act, 2009 (the RTE Act, 2009) was passed (and came into force on 1 April 2010), but its execution has been far from exemplary. Political promises are many, but the political will appears to be weak; lack of resources is often cited as a cause. But we have entered the twenty-first century and India's children cannot wait endlessly and remain ignorant. Their needs have to be dealt with today. The Supreme Court gave children the right to elementary education as part of their right to a dignified life and thus to a life where they can make choices, as far back as 1993. This is the law of the land which has now been endorsed by Section 21A of the Constitution and the RTE Act, 2009, and it must be implemented immediately and effectively.

Does the Convention on the Rights of the Child make a difference to the condition of children in a place like India? Yes, if it is not treated as a substitute for action but as a 'legal lever' to arouse social consciousness and to promote, pursue and push these rights in order that mankind gives the child the best it can. In fact, as mentioned earlier, the monitoring mechanism provided in the convention regarding each ratifying state reporting to the committee certainly leads to some element of accountability.

It is difficult to break the vicious circle of child labour, since most of it occurs in the unorganized sector. However, it can be broken if compulsory primary education is properly implemented, as it is easier to keep track of whether a child is going to a school than whether he is working. What we have to ensure is that education is made attractive so that the child not only enrols but also stays on in school. As stated in *Lalima Gupta and Others vs State of Himachal Pradesh and Another,* the best way to educate small children is for the school to be an extension of the home, so that children can develop in a natural and holistic manner.

Now with the convention having been ratified by India and the passage of the Right to Education Act, the future of India's children appears to be somewhat brighter—at least in principle, work should not be allowed to interfere with primary education. As a UNICEF representative in

India has said, education is 'the most effective strategy for promoting social equality' and 'basic education is the single most critical plank of the infrastructure required for economic growth. No country has been able to alleviate mass poverty without removing mass illiteracy.'

Another relevant aspect of the issue is that at the Vienna Human Rights Conference in June 1993, the US administration made it clear that it would ban the import of products made by child labour. In 1996 Senator Tom Harkin reintroduced the Child Labour Deterrence Bill (first proposed in 1992) that prohibits the import into the USA of goods made wholly or partly by children under 15 years of age. Europe also implemented similar laws. This naturally affects the carpet industry, as 90 per cent of the carpets made in India are presently exported. So the Carpet Export Promotion Council, feeling threatened by the possibility of this ban, decided to adopt a voluntary code of conduct to eliminate the use of child labour. Recent reports, however, suggest that the practice is still rampant and that children are still being used and exploited in the industry.

It is also important to mention the International Labour Organization's convention, which was introduced after a global march and a convergence of delegates (including children) at Geneva ILO Headquarters after country-level workshops and demonstrations. The resulting Worst Forms of Child Labour Convention (No. 182), with its accompanying Recommendation No. 190, was adopted in 1999. It requires all ratifying members to 'take immediate and effective measures to secure the prohibition and elimination of the worst forms of child labour'. It targets all forms of slavery, child prostitution and the use of children in other illicit activities such as the drug trade; it also talks of work that is likely to harm the health, safety or morals of children. It directs member countries to identify and reach out to children at special risk and to take account of 'the special situation of girls'. No country could possibly disagree with this or the request to prevent or remove children from targeted forms of child labour and to provide education, vocational training, or other viable alternatives to inappropriate work. The convention demands that each member state prepare an action plan and that it seek international cooperation in support of implementation. It strikes a chord in terms of the values of virtually every society.

The accompanying Recommendation 190 provides for taking into consideration the views of the children directly affected by the worst forms of child labour, thus bringing forward the concept contained in the Convention on the Rights of the Child that children are, within reason, competent to act on their own behalf.

Education of all children is essential. They are the parents of tomorrow, and can eliminate dowry, discrimination and other evils, and can also change the attitudes of others. ILO Convention 182, which specifically refers to 'the special situation of girls', is very relevant for India. Compulsory primary education must be enforced to remedy the plight of the girl child in India, for unless her status improves, there is no hope for the future.

The need of the hour is the immediate implementation of compulsory education and the creation of an environment leading to equality. An educated child, especially an educated girl child, will eventually result in an educated family and a just society free from superstition and prejudice. When children play and study together, caste and religious differences don't seem to matter; even economic differences are obliterated when the bonds of friendship flourish.

Apart from this, an educated woman will be anxious to implement family planning, health care and sanitation; she will have the capacity to earn and thus not feel suppressed and subordinate to men. She will be self-confident and not view marriage as her only option, thus, hopefully, resulting in the decline and death of the evils of dowry, female foeticide and infanticide. An educated woman is an empowered person and will help to reduce gender bias. She will ensure that both boys and girls go to school rather than to underage work.

Of the approximately 114 million out-of-school children in India, 80 per cent are girls. Further, only about five million children are covered by the narrow definition of child labour, which is a gross underestimation. This is because working children who are not wage earners but either supplement family labour or else work in the unorganized sector are not taken into consideration when estimating the figures of child labour. Child labourers are present both in urban and rural areas. They work as rag pickers, in abattoirs, on construction sites, in hotels and shops, as sex workers, domestic workers, agricultural workers and so on. They can be seen everywhere: on the streets, in the factories, in homes and in the fields.

So primary education must be looked upon as a legal duty, not just a right. It must be implemented by the state with all speed. The education must be holistic, value based and environment friendly. The state's excuse of a lack of sufficient funds is not acceptable. As Indira Gandhi pointed out, the cost of one missile is equivalent to 65,000 schools. It is the duty of the state to provide quality education to its children. The state cannot betray their trust. The future of the world is dependent on today's children, and it is the task of the educator to ensure that they learn the difference between good and evil and, as educator Maria Montessori said, 'not confound good with immobility and evil with activity'.

The Census Report 2011 shows that literacy in India is now at 73 per cent. This improvement is even more significant when one realizes that female literacy has increased from 54.2 per cent in 2001 to 64.6 per cent in 2011. It is also interesting to observe that consequently the male–female difference in literacy rates has consequently declined from 21.7 per cent in 2001 to 16.3 per cent in 2011. The gap in literacy rates between men and women has declined in urban and rural areas.

The best news relates to the state of Himachal Pradesh and is contained in the Public Report on Basic Education in India (PROBE survey 2006). It reports spectacular progress from a low base, with 60 per cent of women and 75 per cent of men having more than five years of education in Himachal Pradesh in 2006 (compared to 40 per cent and 57 per cent respectively for India as a whole). The growth in literacy can partly be attributed to the fact that a large number of women work outside the home. But the change has mainly come about owing to the exceptionally high parental motivation for education in Himachal Pradesh and the government's efforts and spending priorities. The parents' passion for child education was a result of their perception that it helped a person to stand for panchayat elections, do bank work, travel anywhere without fear and generally participate with confidence in a modern society. They also believed that girls have the same capabilities as boys and can become teachers and doctors and useful members of society. They had a broad understanding of the value of education.

The example of Himachal Pradesh indicates that with public initiative, priority spending and parental passion, even 'wobbly' government schools can be brought to life. So there is hope of a real breakthrough, and a belief that change can be brought about even in states like Bihar, Madhya Pradesh, Rajasthan and Uttar Pradesh. It is clear that child labour is employed on a massive scale in India mainly because the system has failed to provide for and enforce the basic right to free and compulsory primary education. But there is some movement towards this. Appreciating that they are two sides of the same coin, the Andhra Pradesh government has merged the two previously separate departments of education and labour. Also, after a long struggle against government servants employing children as domestic servants, the Government of India finally issued a notification on 14 October 1999 that if a government servant employs a child under 14 years of age, it will be considered misconduct, attracting a major penalty under the Central Civil Services (Conduct) Rules, 1964.

Child labour deprives children of educational opportunities, stunts their growth both physically and intellectually, and forces them to continue living a life of drudgery and degradation. Children need leisure and laughter to grow, and their lost innocence can never be given back. So let us strive to see that the promises of the convention and those of our own Constitution become a living reality for every child. Literacy will liberate children from their 'tremendous sense of powerlessness' and socialization in school will reduce inequalities based on caste, class and gender.

The PROBE report has pointed out that all over the country there is an overwhelming popular demand for elementary education of decent quality. It says, 'The time is for concerned action. The future of hundreds of millions of children is at stake.' Not only must we ensure good infrastructure and full enrolment, but also better learning. We must do this in order to achieve quality education to promote gender equity, and to eradicate child labour. We must empower children by freeing them and we must free children by empowering them.

The Girl Child

Rabindranath Tagore said, 'Every time a child is born, it brings with it the hope that God is not yet disappointed with man'. But it appears to me that when a girl child is born in India, more often than not, man is disappointed with God. The birth of the first daughter is often considered bad luck, the second a disaster and the third a catastrophe. The *Atharva Veda*, in fact, seems to enforce this: 'The birth of a girl, grant it elsewhere, here grant a boy.' (VI-2-3)

The Constitution of India not only grants equality to women but also empowers the state to adopt measures of affirmative discrimination in favour of women. The Constitution further imposes a duty on every citizen to renounce practices derogatory to the dignity of women. But, as is apparent, girls in our society don't get the benefit of this fundamental right. On the one hand, women are worshipped as devis and, on the other, female foetuses are indiscriminately destroyed. A survey done in Mumbai in 1984 found that out of 8,000 abortions, 7,999 were female foetuses. This continuing foeticide over the years has resulted in an adverse sex ratio in the country, with

914 females per 1000 males (according to the 2011 census), down from 972 in 1901. There are about 7.1 million fewer girls than boys in the age group of 0-6 years. The normal natural child-sex ratio at birth is 100 females to 106 males; but as the male baby is genetically fragile, this balances out. The highest adverse ratios in India are in Haryana: 120, Punjab: 118 and Jammu and Kashmir: 116.

With the advent of ultrasound technology, female foeticide has taken over from female infanticide as a way of getting rid of the girl child. In order to put a stop to this evil, an Act was passed. The Pre-Conception and Pre-Natal Diagnostic Techniques (Prohibition of Sex Selection) Act, 1994, implemented in 1996, popularly known as PCPNDT Act, bans the use of diagnostic techniques for determining the sex of the foetus. Unfortunately, this Act has had hardly any effect on preventing the misuse of techniques to prevent prenatal sex determination. One reason is that there have been very few prosecutions and convictions of doctors and technicians. Another is that a great deal of primary health care is unregulated and private. But the main reason is that we have not been able to change the preference for sons that is deep-rooted in the minds of most Indian families. Once the sex of the foetus is known, if it is female, the desire to abort it is strong.

The government has sought to influence parental preference by conditional cash transfer (CCT) schemes such as Beti Hai Anmol, Dhan Lakshmi, Ladli etc. These are based on the concept that in order to get the incentive, families have to ensure birth registration, school enrolment, adequate attendance, immunization, prenatal and postnatal healthcare treatment and delaying the age of marriage till after 18 years.

The International Institute for Population Sciences, along with the United Nations Population Fund, did a study which indicated that these schemes were not very effective owing to the many conditions attached, the documentation required, and the bureaucracy involved. The study found that the adverse female child ratio prevailed not only in poorer families but in families of every economic class.

One of the schemes for improving the sex ratio, in Himachal Pradesh, is known as the Indira Gandhi Balika Suraksha Yojana. It has the dual aim of promoting small families and encouraging gender equality. It requires the family to furnish an affidavit attested by an executive magistrate stating that they have one or two female children (and no male child) when accepting the terminal sterilization method.

Schemes such as this raise complex issues. On the one hand is the girl child's right to be born; and on the other, there is the question of a woman's reproductive rights—that is, the right to safe and legal abortion under the Medical Termination of Pregnancy Act, 1971 (as amended in 1975). The government may not be getting the best results because it has been conflating the two different ideas—of small families and of female equity.

But how does one instil in parents the idea that a girl

is as good as a boy? Girls are certainly as caring, if not more, of their parents; but in India the perception that a son provides support in old age persists. An educated, empowered girl can be as much of a support as a son and can even perform the funeral rites. This idea has to be drummed into the minds of men in particular, as this is the prime source of the great pressure on women to produce sons. Men should also be made aware that it is the sperm from the male that determines the sex of the child.

My father, who always treated me in the same manner as my brothers, used to refer to me and not his sons, as 'mere budhape ki lakri'. Unfortunately, he died young, and I could not be the support and walking stick of his old age.

The ideology of patriarchy and the accompanying culture of silence need to be challenged and broken if development is to touch the lives of women. An empowerment strategy can only be effective if patriarchal perceptions are altered and an expanding network of support services built up to free women from some of their own assumed gender-related shackles.

We can only change the popular mindset by campaigning and influencing communities and by implementing the law vigorously. Women must be a part of the decision-making in this regard. In 2012, over 200 women in a Haryana village (appropriately called Bibipur) took part in a panchayat along with men and passed a resolution that female foeticide is a heinous act and should be treated as murder.

Ritu Jaglan, a post graduate from the village and her brother Sunil Jaglan, a mathematics graduate and the sarpanch of the village of Bibipur, were the driving forces behind the campaign. Over a period of two years they mobilized and sensitized the villagers through plays, rallies and door-to-door campaigns. The village now takes pride in families that only have daughters. The dynamic young sarpanch motivated Anganwadi workers (who focus on the health and education needs of young children) Santosh and Asha Rani to go from house to house, spreading the message that daughters are as precious as sons and as capable of carrying on the family lineage. They also pointed out the health hazards of foeticide. This resulted in a change of mindset among the villagers. It is a model which can be replicated in other villages. In fact, neighbouring villages in Haryana, Rajasthan, Uttar Pradesh, Delhi and Punjab have already been influenced by this example. This social change is now being brought about by the people themselves.

It is only when people feel that *they* have taken a decision that they feel responsible for ensuring that it is implemented. This was certainly a big step forward for Bibipur, and the chief minister responded very quickly by announcing a one crore rupee development package for the village. He said that though the state had a number of schemes to check the menace of female foeticide, the issue needed the whole-hearted support of the people.

This was no small achievement, but a lot remains

to be done. What is clear is that the government must collaborate with the people to save, nurture and educate the girl child. The government's intentions may be laudable, but what we really want is action resulting in the economic and emotional empowerment of the girl child. Further, the incentives should be easily accessible and the political will to ensure gender equity must never falter.

■

Why is a daughter considered a curse? Mainly because she is seen as an economic liability: the difficulties faced by parents in getting her married without an adequate dowry are considerable. This results in parents treating their sons and daughters differently: loving one and neglecting the other; doting on the son and depriving the daughter; educating the boy and letting the girl child remain unlettered while making her do domestic chores, including looking after the siblings and cattle.

As a result of the preference for a son, the unwanted girl is neglected, and receives poorer quality of food, health care, clothing and education. This stunts her growth; she cannot get empowered mentally or be as strong as her brother physically. The 'son preference' in our country is encapsulated in expressions and blessings like, 'May you be the mother of a thousand sons'. We have to get rid of all this.

In South Korea, which was a rigidly patriarchal society, there has been a change in thinking. Apart from promoting socio-economic development and changing the laws of inheritance, etc., a multi-pronged attack was mounted to deal with the issue, and campaigns featured popular slogans like, 'One daughter raised well is worth ten sons'.

How do we change this patriarchal mindset in India? Changing the laws and making sure they are properly implemented is one aspect of it. But that is not enough. The law is only a springboard from which to take off. Altering the mindset is crucial. It is the implementation of the law and the way in which the community adopts it that are most relevant. What the girl child is asking for is not extraordinary. All she wants is a fair deal: the right to be born; the right to be nourished and loved; the right to be no worse than any boy; the right to choose; and the right to excel. In brief, she wants equity, self-esteem and dignity. To achieve this, we need to mount a multi-pronged attack. And we need to use advocacy.

The most important tool for bringing about attitudinal changes is education. This means the education of all children. It is they who are the parents of tomorrow and can eliminate social evils such as of dowry and discrimination. In fact, the education of girls and women is a necessity, as it is only then that they can be aware of their rights, assert them and change perceptions in society, both for themselves and for their children.

Tradition cannot be used as an excuse for delay. The girl child cannot wait silently till tomorrow.

At the beginning of the twentieth century, there was hardly any provision in India for the formal education of girls. In 1901, the literacy rate amongst women was only 0.8 per cent. The number of girls enrolled for every hundred boys was only twelve at the primary stage and four at the secondary stage. The total enrolment in higher education was only 264, which included seventy-six girls studying in medical colleges and eleven in colleges of education.

Since 1951, there has been a steady growth in female literacy and as of 2011 it stands at 64.6 per cent. There are, however, wide regional variations ranging from near universal literacy in Kerala to 47.76 per cent female literacy in Rajasthan. The change from the previous census has taken place because rural-urban differentials in literacy have declined.

According to the 8th All India School Education Survey of the NCERT (National Council of Educational Research and Training), while female enrolment at the primary stage was 48.13 per cent, it came down to 42.56 per cent at the higher secondary stage. While enrolment has been growing over the years, the end result is not entirely satisfactory. This is because of the high dropout rate, which continues to be a major problem. The dropout rate for girls has decreased when compared to a few decades ago, but even now nearly half the girls who enrol in school do not complete their education. One of the biggest causes for this high rate of dropout is child marriage. A girl is considered paraya dhan—another's wealth—and is seen as a transitory member of her natal family. Her whole upbringing is oriented towards getting her married off. Her education is considered unnecessary and often an impediment to keeping her subservient and 'marriageable'.

Although social pressures might act to keep a girl uneducated, the right to primary education was held to be a fundamental right as far back as 1993. In *Unni Krishnan J.P. and Others vs State of Andhra Pradesh and Others*, three out of the five judges expressed their opinion that though the right to education is not stated expressly as a fundamental right, it is implicit in and flows from the right to life guaranteed under Article 21, as education is of paramount importance for living a worthwhile life. Consequently, construing Articles 41, 45 and 46 of the Directive Principles of Part IV of the Constitution, the Supreme Court held that every child/citizen of this country has a right to free education until he completes the age of 14; thereafter, his rights are circumscribed by the state's economic capacity and development. Subsequently, the Constitution was amended (86th Amendment Act, 2002) and Article 21A introduced, which reads: 'The State shall provide free and compulsory education to all children of the age of six to fourteen years in such manner as the State may, by law, determine.' Thereafter, the Right of Children to Free and Compulsory Education Act, 2009 (RTE Act, 2009) was passed; it came into force on 1 April 2010.

Owing to the recognition of this fundamental right and a slow improvement in attitudes, more girls are now getting an education. This has led to greater employment opportunities, which in turn have played a role in raising their age at marriage. But there is still a long way to go.

In India, child marriage was made illegal by the Child Marriage Restraint Act in 1929. The defined marriageable ages were 15 for a girl and 18 for a boy. In 1978, through an amendment, this age was increased to 18 for girls and 21 for boys. But child marriages continued to take place with impunity. So in 2006 the Child Marriage Prohibition Act was passed; this made the solemnization of child marriage a cognizable and non-bailable offence. Yet even now child marriages continue; they are more prevalent in rural than urban areas. In some states like Rajasthan, mass child marriages used to take place on Akshaya Tritiya day. The Act includes a specific provision to prevent such marriages and the District Magistrate has been made the Child Marriage Prohibition Officer. But, for political reasons, implementation has not been as effective as it should be.

It is said that India has 40 per cent of the world's child brides and that 46 per cent of women in India are married before the age of 18. The human rights NGO Breakthrough, which works in Gaya district in Bihar and Hazaribagh and Ranchi districts in Jharkhand, reported that over 60 per cent of women between the ages of 20 to 24 had been married before the age of 18. Studies by the United Nations Population Fund further say that if these trends continue between 2011 and 2020, more than 140 million girls will become child brides, of which at least 18.5 million will be under the age of 15.

According to a youth survey, three out of ten men

and four out of ten young women did not know that 18 is the minimum legal age for marriage for a female. Further, 91 per cent of young women, regardless of marital status or rural–urban residence, said that they would prefer to marry after the age of 18. A quarter of young women reported that their first sexual experience within marriage had been forced. Further, one in ten young men and one in four young women reported that their parents did not seek their approval when determining their marriage partner.

Article 16 of the Universal Declaration of Human Rights stipulates that marriages should occur only 'with the free and full consent of the intending spouses'. India is a signatory to international conventions that ban child marriage. Child marriage denies a girl her basic human rights and is a blatant violation of the rights of a child as provided in our Constitution. It acts against everything worthwhile: a free and joyful childhood, education, development, participation, health, equality, employment and a dignified life.

Some aspects pertaining to child marriage are frightening and have been referred to as 'children having children and dying'. Girls below the age of 15 are five times more likely to die in childbirth, and girls between the ages of 15 to 19 are twice as likely to die in childbirth as compared to women in their twenties. In addition, girls below the age of 18 are also at much higher risk of pregnancy-related morbidity.

The children of child brides are 60 per cent more

likely to die before their first birthday as compared to children of mothers who are over 19. Child brides are at greater risk of contracting HIV and other sexually-transmitted diseases. Child marriage also affects a girl's education and her right to equal opportunity or economic empowerment. Thus it hinders six of the UN's eight Millennium Development Goals: eradication of extreme poverty and hunger; achieving universal primary education; promoting gender equality and empowerment of women; reducing child mortality; improving maternal health; and combating HIV/AIDS, malaria and other diseases.

The 2001 Indian census indicated that 300,000 girls under 15 had given birth, some for the second time. But why was child marriage so prevalent in the past and why does it still continue, though to a much smaller extent, even today? The answer lies in the patriarchal system and the socialization process in India, which works to make boys independent and to get girls married. Traditionally a girl is not supposed to do anything independently. When she attains puberty, she becomes sexually vulnerable and requires protection. Her parents want to shift this burden as soon as possible, and marriage is considered a priority. Since she is not educated, she is dependent on others. All this is what society envisages and expects.

This has been the position from the ancient times of Manu who pronounces in the *Manusmriti*:

> *She should do nothing independently*
> *even in her own house;*

in childhood, subject to her father;
in youth to her husband;
and when her husband is dead to her son;
she should never enjoy independence...

But more than sixty years ago, Rabindranath Tagore questioned the inequality of the situation in the following words:

O Lord, why have you not given
Woman the right to conquer her destiny?
Why does she have to wait,
Head bowed, by the roadside,
Waiting with tired patience,
Hoping for a miracle on the morrow?

Has that morrow now arrived and is that miracle now taking place?

Traditionally, the attainment of puberty has played an important role in determining the age of marriage for girls. Despite this, the mean age of marriage for females, which was 13.2 years at the beginning of the twentieth century, rose to 16.1 during 1951–1961. The average age went up to 17.2 years by 1971 and 18.3 by 1981.

By 1992, the mean age of 'effective marriage' for females was 19.5. In that year more than 90 per cent of women were married by the age of 29 years, though about 30 per cent of them were married while still in their teens, i.e. between the ages of 15 and 19. By 2011 the mean age of marriage for females had increased to

22.2, but 61 per cent of women are married before they are 16 and are pregnant for the first time by the time they are 19.

As mentioned earlier, the Child Marriage Restraint (Amendment) Act, 1978 (Act 2 of 1978) raised the minimum age of marriage of girls to 18 years from 15 and for boys to 21 years from 18, which is what they had been in the Child Marriage Restraint Act, 1929. The intention of the 1929 Act was to prevent child marriages and of the 1978 Amendment to strike at the evil of early marriages of girls and the consequent pregnancies that resulted in undue strain on young mothers and the birth of premature babies. Despite the law, however, child marriages continue.

The Child Marriage and Restraint Act, 1929 applies to all religions but it does not make marriages which are performed below the minimum age null and void. It provides for a punishment for the parents, for the guardians and for the bridegroom, if he is an adult, as also for persons who conduct, perform or direct a child marriage. The question of annulment, repudiation, divorce, etc., however, depends on the personal law of the parties, which depends on their religion.

■

Durgabai Deshmukh was a young woman of great courage and determination who created institutions that helped women at the grass roots. India's search for an organizational structure to coordinate efforts towards gender equality and gender equity began with the establishment of the Central Social Welfare Board in 1953. Durgabai Deshmukh was the woman responsible for its conception and she was appointed its first chairman. The concept of a national machinery has been evolving ever since.

In 1971, the government appointed a Committee on the Status of Women in India. This committee raised basic questions about the socialization process inherent in a hierarchical society. These related to the distribution pattern of power and resources as well as the diverse cultural values in the country. Its report, 'Towards Equality', led to a recognizable shift in attitude—from viewing women as targets of welfare policies in the social sector to regarding them as a critical group for the purposes of development. This was reflected in the Sixth Five Year Plan (1980–1985) which, for the first time in India's planning history, contained a chapter on Women and Development. It conceived of a multi-pronged strategy as essential for women's development in relation to:

- employment and economic independence;
- education;
- access to health care and family planning;
- support services to meet the practical gender needs of women; and
- the creation of an enabling policy, institutional structure and legal environment.

A Department of Women and Child Development was set up in 1985 under the newly created Ministry of Human

Resource Development. One of the most significant institutions set up in 1990 by an Act of Parliament is the National Commission for Women.

The Eighth Five Year Plan (1992–1997) promised to ensure that the benefits of development from different sectors would not bypass women. Consequently, the three core sectors of employment, education and health care were to be monitored very closely. The approach of the Eighth Plan, which regarded women as equal partners in the development process, marked a progress from the goal of development to that of empowerment of women.

The 73rd and 74th Constitutional Amendment Acts of 1993 constituted a watershed for the advancement of Indian women. They ensured that one-third of the total elected seats and positions of chairpersons in rural and urban local bodies would go to women. About one million women were estimated to emerge as leaders at the grass-roots level in the rural areas alone, and of these, 75,000 would be chairpersons.

The Twelfth Five Year Plan (2012–2017) enumerates the following as key elements for gender equality:

- economic empowerment;
- social and physical infrastructure;
- enabling legislations;
- women's participation in governance;
- inclusiveness of all categories of vulnerable women;

- engendering national policies/programmes; and
- mainstreaming gender through gender budgeting.

One of the initiatives of the Twelfth Plan was to build transformative leadership through training and capacity building schemes among minority communities on a large scale, especially among minority women and youth, so that they can themselves create accountability at the local level to help the state provide better neighbourhoods, jobs, education, health, housing, hygiene, skills and incomes.

The government has also appointed a High Level Committee on the Status of Women, which is yet to give its report.

Despite initiatives in every plan, women still comprise the largest section of population living in absolute poverty and represent the poorest of the poor. Despite the specific schemes and programmes of the government, despite the enthusiasm and activities of voluntary agencies, the benefits of development have not yet reached women and girl children. Gender equality is still a distant dream.

The young girl is most vulnerable to the insults of poverty and deprivation. As an infant, she is likely to be breastfed for a shorter time than her brother and be neglected when she falls ill. As she grows up, she becomes the victim of discrimination with regard to access to education, skill development and recreation. Her entire socialization tends to make marriage the ultimate goal of her existence, and subservience to the males in the household both her initial and her final destiny.

The mother and wife, who is required to take care of the physical needs of others, seldom has time to develop her own higher faculties. Women have carried out domestic work for centuries without being given any credit for it. Men have not changed their lifestyles and have been brought up to expect service and care as an integral part of domestic life. Consequently, any women who have tried to achieve something in other spheres have had to make most of the adjustments themselves and have carried out their domestic work alongside any outside work they have done. Now that women are realizing their own potential, domestic work has to be shared. Otherwise there cannot be any equality of opportunity.

Much has changed for the girl child over the past few decades, but not nearly enough. I am hopeful that things will improve faster now. As Victor Hugo said, 'There is one thing stronger than all the armies in the world, and that is an idea whose time has come'.

Widows' Rights

Dressed in white, with her head shaved, glass bangles broken, her sindoor rubbed out, the widow in India, especially amongst Hindus, is considered inauspicious. To appreciate the problems that a widow faces, it is essential to understand her position in society, her economic status and her state of empowerment. It is also necessary to look at customary law, statutory law and actual practice. Though customary law and statutory law might give a widow certain rights, in actual practice none of these rights may be effective because she is not socially empowered to assert those rights and fight for them. It is in this context that one needs to look at the historical background and the present position.

Widows in all communities carried the stigma of being inauspicious and were not allowed to participate in religious or auspicious social functions such as marriage or other celebrations. A widow was not even allowed to perform the ritual ceremony to welcome her own daughter-in-law into the home. This ostracism and labelling as an ill-omen took place despite the fact that many of the widows were very young girls whose marriage had not even been consummated. Often the mother-in-law blamed her for her son's death. The death of the husband was the start of a young woman's problems. She was either expected to commit sati or to go back to her parents. But if she stayed with her husband's family she had to do all the menial work, was ill-treated and not even given proper food. A widow was not allowed to make herself attractive as she was considered a sexual threat to society. She was made to eat vegetarian food and in Uttar Pradesh, I know, she was not even allowed to eat masur dal, onions and garlic as they were considered 'heating'. A widow who remained chaste and did not remarry was considered tolerable. Consequently, widow remarriage was not permitted amongst Hindus, especially among Brahmins and higher caste communities.

Widow remarriage was and is still prevalent among tribal communities, however, even if Hindu. In fact, among such communities, levirate marriages were very common, that is, a widow remarrying her husband's unmarried younger brother. This entitled the widow to retain her right over her children and her late husband's property. In certain communities, for example, Bhumij tribals in West Bengal, if a widow decided to marry someone other than her deceased husband's younger brother, she forfeited not only her right to her husband's property but also her children, as the husband's family would insist that she leave her children with them.

But among Hindus in general, a widow was not allowed to have a second marriage unless it was sanctioned by local or caste custom. Even if permitted, however, it entailed the forfeiture or divesting of the widow's estate (i.e., the estate that she inherited from her husband) in most cases. This was because there was a settled rule of Hindu law that chastity was a 'condition precedent' for a widow to inherit property from her husband. By the same reasoning, she would not be entitled to the widow's estate if there had been sexual infidelity in his lifetime, unless he had condoned it.

Remarriage of widows was legalized in all cases by the Hindu Widows Remarriage Act, 1856. But the Act provided that all rights and interest which a widow had in her deceased husband's estate would 'cease and determine' on her remarriage as if she had died. This Act of 1856 was repealed by the Hindu Widows Remarriage (Repeal) Act, 1983 on the recommendation of the 81st Report of the Law Commission of India. However, even earlier, she could inherit the estate of a deceased son or daughter from her first marriage even if she had remarried.

The Hindu Women's Right to Property Act, 1937 gave better rights to a Hindu woman in respect of property than she had earlier, but in the form of a limited estate to be held by her only during her lifetime, reverting upon her death to her husband's heirs. Later, by virtue of Section 14(1) of the Hindu Succession Act, 1956, a widow's limited interest was automatically converted into an absolute right. It is now judicially settled that once a widow has succeeded to her husband's property, she cannot be divested of this right on remarriage.

In order to understand the law relating to a widow's property rights, we need to appreciate that inheritance and property rights are governed by the personal laws of the different religious communities and vary from area to area even among communities and castes. Among Hindus there are two kinds of property: (i) self-acquired property and (ii) ancestral/joint family property. There are two major schools of Hindu law governing ancestral property—the Dayabhaga and the Mitakshara. The Dayabhaga law prevails in eastern India in states like West Bengal and other adjoining areas, whereas in most of northern India and parts of western India, it is the Mitakshara law that prevails. In certain parts of western India the Mayukha school is prevalent, whereas in some parts of southern India the Marumakkattayam, Aliyasantana and the Nambudri laws prevail.

In the Dayabhaga system persons held the property as tenants in common. When the father died, the property was divided between the heirs and they could hold it together if they wanted, but their shares were defined. Under the Mitakshara system a male member of the joint family had an interest by birth in the ancestral property. A man could ask for partition of his ancestral property but if he did not, his interest in the ancestral property was diverted to all male members of the coparcenary when he died. It went to them by survivorship and not succession. Women were not coparceners and did not have any interest by birth in the ancestral property. They were only entitled to maintenance, i.e., expenses for food, shelter, clothing, education and marriage of children. However, if partition took place between the male members, then mothers and wives were entitled to a limited interest for the purposes of maintenance and, on their death, the share reverted to the husband's or son's heirs. They were not entitled to sell, mortgage or will away that property.

The Hindu Succession Act, 1956 was a comprehensive law covering the various systems. It brought about some major changes. The most important changes were to give equal rights to sons and daughters in their father's and mother's property; and to abolish the concept of a widow's estate that gave her only a limited life estate and convert it into an absolute right. If a Hindu male died without making a will, his share would be divided among his heirs, his four primary heirs being his sons, daughters, widow and mother; the others are derivative heirs, i.e., children of a pre-deceased son or pre-deceased daughter, widowed daughter-in-law and children of a pre-deceased grandson and his widow. But it did not do away with the concept of coparcenary in ancestral (i.e. joint family) property, nor did it give the daughter a right by birth in this ancestral property. However, a Hindu male became entitled to will away his interest in the ancestral property. With respect to his self-acquired property, a Hindu male was entitled to will it away even before the Hindu Succession Act, 1956.

By virtue of Section 14(1) of the Hindu Succession Act, 1956, women became absolute owners of the property they inherited. They could sell it, gift it, mortgage it, spend it or waste it. After a woman's death, her property would be divided amongst her heirs. A female's heirs are different to a male's heirs. In the first class they are sons, daughters and husband.

The Supreme Court, in *Raghubir Singh and Others vs Gulab Singh and Others*, held that a right to maintenance of a Hindu female flows from the social and temporal relationship between the husband and wife and that right in the case of a widow is a pre-existing right under shastric Hindu law even before the passing of the Hindu Women's Right to Property Act, 1937, and the Hindu Married Women's Rights to Separate Residence and Maintenance Act, 1946. These acts only recognized the position as existing under shastric Hindu Law and gave it a 'statutory' backing. Thus if a Hindu widow is in possession of the property of her husband, she has a right to be maintained out of it and is entitled to retain the possession of that property in lieu of her right to maintenance.

The Supreme Court followed the earlier case of *Vaddeboyina Tulasamma vs V. Sesha Reddi (Dead) by L.Rs.* and *Ram Kali vs Choudhri Ajit Shankar*, and held that by force of Section 14(1) of the Hindu Succession Act, 1956, the widow's limited interest gets automatically enlarged into an absolute right notwithstanding any restriction placed under the document or instrument. Section 14(2), however, applies to instruments, decrees, awards, gifts, etc., which create an independent or new title in favour of the female heir for the first time.

In April 2013, a Division Bench of the Punjab and Haryana High Court held that a Hindu widow need not be in actual physical possession to become an absolute owner.

Under Muslim law a male can only will away one-third of his property. A widow is entitled to one-eighth of her husband's property if there are children, and to one-fourth if there are no children. If a man has two widows they would inherit one-eighth or one-fourth depending on whether or not there are children. A daughter is entitled to half of her father's property if she has no brother. If she has a brother she will get half of whatever share the brother gets. The mother is entitled to one-third of her son's property if he doesn't have any children and one-sixth if he has children.

In practice, among both Muslims and Hindus, the widow's place of residence is crucial to the exercise of her legal right. A widow will, in practice, get her share of property as long as she lives in her marital home but not if she remarries. Despite the fact that widow re-marriage is permitted by Islam, it is somehow not considered 'respectful' to take up this option. A Muslim widow clearly had inheritance rights in her parental home as a daughter but, in practice, as among Hindus, daughters were not given anything. If a Muslim woman insisted on taking her share, she would no longer be welcome in her parental home and would have to break off relationships with her brothers. But on being widowed she could stay in her parental home as a dependent in case she was not able to do so in her marital home.

It is important to see how widows—of any community—regard themselves with respect to property, what their social perceptions are and how aware they are of the law. People take recourse to statutory law only when there is a dispute, but normally widows do not like raising disputes and want to live in harmony, especially as they feel socially dependent. They like to practise what is in keeping with the norms of the community. They feel that a widow's rightful home is with her husband's family and all her rights are in her marital home. A widow does not want to assert her rights as a daughter in her father's home for fear of spoiling relationships all around.

As a judge, I have come across daughters giving affidavits in courts relinquishing their right in favour of their brothers upon their father's death. When I questioned them, I found that they were aware of their rights but relinquished them in the interest of maintaining harmony with their brothers—something they valued more than the property.

Widows are often willing to forfeit their property rights in favour of their adult sons, who they expect will look after them. But a widow with minor sons typically claims the rights in her husband's property and a widow with daughters, with some difficulty, manages to claim her rights too. A childless widow, however, finds it very difficult to do so because the community does not perceive it as her social right. Thus, though in principle the widow has the right and she is aware of it, in practice her rights have become limited and restricted either because her father-in-law refuses to give her a share of the property or because her brothers-in-law decide to act tough or because her adult sons will not allow her a share. This is based on the old conception that a widow was given property rights to enable her to maintain her sons. That is why she was originally given only limited usufructory rights to use the property while her son was a minor. But even women who know the present law and know that they have substantial rights are not willing to meet the officials or to go to court to assert their rights. As I have noted above, if their share is not given to them in their father's home voluntarily, they do not want to go to court for this purpose and, in effect, relinquish their rights.

A young widow is viewed as an adversary and the mother-in-law often taunts her for being responsible for her son's death. Her own parents usually try to provide emotional support and help to ensure that she gets her share of property but prefer that she stay on in her marital home rather than come back to them. The ideal widows according to the community appear to be the ones who obey all restrictions placed on them, observe all prescriptions and—in the case of a Hindu woman—wear all symbols of a Hindu widow. The widows are compelled to do this despite the fact that they find it extremely difficult to earn a living while remaining imprisoned within the four walls of their houses. They cannot work outside, eat nourishing food or dress up because this would supposedly tempt the males of their husband's village.

With regard to remarriage, the perception is that unmarried men do not like to marry a widow, while a widower can easily get an unmarried young girl as a second or third wife. However, if it comes to it, a childless widow is preferred for remarriage to one with children.

Until a few years ago, the family pension given to widows of army personnel (war widows) was discontinued on her re-marriage unless she married her late husband's brother. This was unjust. A similar unfairness existed in the case of an army person who remarried after retirement. In the event of his death his widow did not get the family pension. The explanation for this was that she was not his wife when he was in service. Mohini Giri, Chairperson of the Guild for Service, as well as members of other organizations, lobbied to ensure that such rules in the army were changed so that a widow's right to her pension could not be snatched away if she exercised her right to remarry. Ms J. Gurmit Singh, President of the War Widows Association, India, informed me that they had been successful in getting this rule changed a few years ago. This is referred to as a 'special liberalized family pension'.

One of the biggest traumas a widow faces after the death of her husband is the whole question of support or shelter—how and where can she live. If she was living with her in-laws, she is often either thrown out or given such a difficult time that it becomes impossible for her to remain there. If she was living in accommodation provided by the employer of her husband, then that has to be vacated and she has to find a roof over her head. She may or may not be welcome in her parental home and is at the mercy of relatives and others. It is thus essential that some thought be given to this aspect of the matter and some provision for shelter be organized during the lifetime of her husband. If joint family land has been partitioned, then it should be registered in the name of both husband and wife, so that she can continue to look after the fields and support herself and her children after his death.

We need to build social awareness and change the mindset of people towards widows. We need to educate girls so that they can be independent, fend for themselves and fight for their own rights.

Public pressure must also be built up to give widows in this country dignity and respect. Non-governmental organizations must take on the role of social reformers and press ahead to make life easier for them. We have seen how lobbying has been effective in the case of war widows. Training for employment or compensatory job opportunities should be provided. Smaller entrepreneurial units should be made available so that a widow has some means of livelihood and does not have to migrate to Vrindavan or Varanasi as her only resort.

Prisoners' Rights

'Prisons have been such a garbage can of society that they have been a garbage can of the law as well,' said Herman Schwartz, Professor of Law at the American University's Washington College of Law, therein summing up the general position of prisons around the world.

In India we have an archaic law pertaining to prisons. This is the Prison Act of 1894, which is more than 120 years old. Despite almost sixty-seven years of independence and numerous committees and commissions and a plethora of recommendations, not many changes have been brought about to this Act.

Professor Richard B. Lillich, another authority on international law, particularly human rights, asked pertinently, whether the purpose of prisons is to inflict the maximum suffering on the offender or to offer the maximum opportunity for readjustment and self-improvement. Over the years, the approach has radically changed and moved from retribution to deterrence and, subsequently, to rehabilitation and reform.

But in the popular mind, a prisoner is an offender and a threat to society, to law and order, and to personal security; he should be locked away and forgotten. How, people ask, can one talk about prisoners' rights when they are responsible for crimes such as stealing or maiming or killing? The public impulse is that they should be punished—sometimes even kept in fetters. This led the Supreme Court of India to ask, 'Are prisoners persons?' And answer: 'Yes, of course. To answer in the negative is to convict the nation and the Constitution of dehumanization and to repudiate the world legal order, which now recognizes rights of prisoners in the International Covenant on Prisoners' Rights, to which our country has signed assent.'

The Supreme Court added: 'Prisoners are peculiarly and doubly handicapped. For one thing, most prisoners belong to the weaker segment, in poverty, illiteracy, social station and the like. Secondly, the prison house is a walled-off world which is incommunicado for the human world, with the result that the bonded inmates are invisible, their voices inaudible, their injustices unheeded.'

The court held that prisoners are entitled to every freedom not necessitated by incarceration and sentence—that is, the freedom to read and write; to exercise, meditate and chant; to move within the prison campus and enjoy the minimal joys of self-expression; to acquire skills and techniques within the limitation of imprisonment; and to be protected from indignities and the extremities of weather.

Since Independence, various committees, starting with the All India Jail Manual Committee 1957–1959 and going on to the All India Committee on Jail Reforms, 1980–1983 chaired by former Justice A. N. Mulla (subsequently referred to as the Mulla Committee), have suggested reforms to incorporate the new approach.

One of the major problems in prisons all over the world has been overcrowding, which affects the right to live with dignity. Though the population of India crossed the billion mark more than a decade ago, the number of prisoners in India is comparatively not large. In 2012, Prison Statistics India showed the number as 385,135 and the authorized capacity as 343,169. Undertrial prisoners constitute 66.2 per cent (254,857) of the total prison population in the country. Some prisons are overcrowded and some comparatively empty. Although prisons is a state subject (Item 4 of State List II of the Seventh Schedule), the problem of overcrowding can be tackled if there is political will and cooperation between states.

Delhi's Central Jail, Tihar, is the largest composite jail in India and South Asia. The sanctioned capacity for this jail including an adjacent camp jail (as per the Mulla Committee Report, 1980–1983) was 1,773 but there were about 3,000 prisoners in the said jail at that time. Even now, the situation is not very different. As of 28 February 2014, Tihar Jail had an authorized capacity of 6,250 (which includes 5,850 males and 400 females) and an inmate population that was more than double that, at 13,836 (13,204 males and 632 females). When the prisoners lodged far exceed the capacity of the prison, extra prisoners have to be accommodated through internal adjustment, which creates numerous administrative and other problems. A great deal of time, money and human suffering is involved in the overuse of prison facilities and it is difficult to balance the requirements of security, control and justice.

Justice Mulla made a strong plea for reducing the overcrowding, as the committee found that undertrials at Tihar constituted 75 per cent to 80 per cent of the jail population. About 200 to 300 undertrials had to go to court every day. A lot of time was spent in handing them over to the police party for attending court and receiving them back in the evening. This provided scope for smuggling articles into and out of the jail as undertrials and convicts were lodged in the same jail and had to pass through the same gate and share the same kitchens, jail hospital, canteen and library facilities. Despite the Mulla Committee findings and recommendations and those of others, undertrials continue to make up the majority of the jailed population at Tihar.

Even in 1996, while examining Rajan Pillai's custodial death (Justice Leila Seth Commission of Inquiry), I had occasion to examine the same jail and observe the consequences of extra prisoners being accommodated through internal adjustment. In the wards, prisoners were sleeping on the floor in between the raised cement platforms or beds and three or more were housed in cells meant for a single individual, resulting in prisoners having to sleep right next to open toilet facilities. Inadequate latrines and toilets attached to the wards were overused to the extent that the condition was totally deplorable despite the Mulla Committee's recommendation that the ratio of latrines to prisoners should be one to six, and that there should be an adequate number of separate urinals and bathing cubicles to ensure privacy, sanitation and hygiene. Where there is more than one inmate in a cell, prisoners have to use the toilet facilities while the others are present. This is certainly not in keeping with human dignity.

There is no doubt that overcrowding results in stretching facilities and services to breaking point. For instance, if a doctor has to medically examine, record and write prescriptions for a hundred patients in three hours, he can hardly spend more than a minute and a half with each patient. This would be a mockery of a medical examination.

There is an Arabic proverb which says: 'He who has health has hope; and he who has hope has everything.' Because prisoners live in very difficult conditions, physically crowded and uncomfortable, mentally isolated and frustrating, they are, therefore, more prone to suffer physical and mental ill health. But they are in the custody of the state and have to be properly attended to, as any negligence on the part of the staff, however unavoidable, will lead to public criticism. Moreover, Article 21 of the Indian Constitution protects the life and liberty of all persons. The Supreme Court of India has held that it incorporates the right to health and the right to live with human dignity. Article 47 of the Constitution requires the state to regard the raising of the level of nutrition and the standard of living of its people and the improvement of public health as amongst its primary duties.

The conditions in many other prisons elsewhere in the world are not very different as Vivien Stern notes in her book, *A Sin Against the Future: Imprisonment in the World* (1998). I have relied on it for much of the information about other countries.

In Rio de Janeiro, most prisoners are in their cells for twenty-three hours a day and the situation is similar in Kyrgyzstan, a small country with a population of about 5.6 million, where the prisoners live in crowded dormitories from which they get out for only an hour's exercise each day and where tuberculosis is a major problem. The Central Prison in Harare in Zimbabwe is also overcrowded. Prisoners live in cells which are so small that all that can fit in is a laid out blanket and a bucket, or in dormitories with not enough space for anyone to stretch out.

A recent report on Brixton Prison in south London, which was built in 1819 and lies just four miles away from the Houses of Parliament, revealed that 751 inmates are crammed into single cells built for only 505; some are awaiting trial while others are serving sentences. They get their food from trolleys and eat in their cells. For a few hours each day, they have the chance to exercise in a yard and go to an education class, do some art and craft work or watch television. For the rest of the day, the majority of prisoners are locked up with other prisoners in a small cell with limited material for reading and limited access to a telephone, though they do have a personal radio for company.

The conditions in Brixton, UK may seem better than in the other three countries, but the basic rule of survival for staff and prisoners is the same. Most prisons also smell the same, with too many ill-washed people in a cramped place, inadequate sanitary facilities and overcooked food.

It is true that the 'slopping out' ritual where prisoners had to live for hours in the same room as buckets or pots holding their bodily waste before they were emptied into overflowing sewers is slowly becoming a thing of the past. But we must understand the high level of tension that overcrowding creates and the diseases it spreads. Both staff and prisoners live with the fear of violence as groups or gangs are organized and the new young prisoners are bullied and brutalized.

In 1973, Stephen Donaldson, then aged 26, found himself in jail in Washington D.C. after getting arrested at a Quaker prayer demonstration at the White House against the bombings in Cambodia. He was subsequently acquitted. During his first night in jail, he was repeatedly gang-raped. He later became the president of the organization—Stop Prisoner Rape. He wrote that in most prisons, rape is an entrenched tradition since prisoners consider it a legitimate way to 'prove their manhood' and to satisfy sexual needs and the brutal desire for power. The organization estimated that some 60,000 unwarranted sexual acts take place behind bars in the United States every day and that in the course of a year hundreds of thousands of adult males in prison and jail, and boys in juvenile and adult facilities become victims. Most of the victims are young, straight and non-violent, unable to defend themselves. Very few of these rapes are reported to prison officials because of the dangers in prison of becoming known as an informer, the humiliation of having to admit what has happened and the fear of being classified as homosexual. The organization Stop Prisoner Rape contends that these men and boys will usually return to the community far more violent and anti-social than before they were raped. As a result of the rape, trauma and rage, some of them will themselves become rapists.

From 1973, Stephen Donaldson fought to convince the court that prison officials should be held liable if a prisoner is raped by other prisoners. In 1994, the US Supreme Court ruled that prison officials are liable if they fail to act when they know that the prisoners are at a substantial risk of being harmed by others.

Despite the efforts of human rights organizations, NGOs, committees and commissions trying and sometimes succeeding in improving some conditions for prisoners, prisons remain a gloomy world cut off from family and friends and controlled by people on whom the prisoner is dependent for food, for medicine, for work, for exercise, for access to the outside world and for opportunities both physical and mental. In the words of Lord Woolf, 'justice does not stop at the prison gates' or as our own Justice

Prisoners' Rights

Krishna Iyer has said: 'a prisoner does not shed his basic constitutional rights at the prison gate.'

But what is the purpose of imprisonment? If it is deterrence, is it effective? Do prisons really work? In this connection, it is necessary to look at the background of imprisonment.

In England, in the eighteenth century, hanging was the most severe penalty. A person was hanged for murder, violence, and even for theft of property over a certain value, house breaking, arson, etc. Flogging and branding were also prevalent. Most punishments took place in public so that a message was sent out that those who transgress would be dealt with in a similar manner. It was only for smaller offences that people were sent to prison.

With time, hanging became less acceptable, but there were still many who were not executed and yet found guilty of a serious crime. They could not be set free and had to be kept somewhere. Many people were transported from England to the American colonies and from India to the Andaman and Nicobar Islands, what was then known as Kala Pani or Black Water. After 1776, when criminals from England could no longer be sent to the American colonies, they were sent to Australia. Men, women and children made terrible journeys in which many died on the way, and others perished in the penal colonies, but some became prosperous citizens of the new country. This was resented by the victims. In 1868, transportation to Australia was finally abandoned.

A new idea of how to punish criminals was slowly

developing, as transportation to other countries was no longer seen as viable. The earlier idea of inflicting pain on the body by banishment or transportation or death or flogging was being replaced by an effort to correct the mind. Two different models of imprisonment were developed in the United States: the 'silent system' and the 'separate system'. In the separate system, when a prisoner arrived at a prison, he entered with a black hood over his head. He was taken to a cell and never left it until he had served his entire sentence. Apart from the prison officers he never saw a human being or heard a human voice. He never heard of his wife or children, home or friends or the life or death of anyone. He was a man buried alive. He did not know in what part of the building he was living and what kind of men were near him. The inhumanity of the 'separate system' was horrific.

The 'silent system', on the other hand, allowed the prisoners to mix with each other while they worked during the day but not to communicate. At the Auburn prison in New York, if a prisoner broke the silence rule, he was whipped. In Britain, since it was impossible to find the money to convert some of the old prison buildings so that prisoners could be kept in single cells, prisoners in solitary confinement were allowed to work in the same room as others, provided there was strict silence, as it was believed that the mind became open to the best impressions in solitude and would then receive those truths and consolation which only Christianity could give. This system was not a success and many prisoners succumbed to madness.

So in the early twentieth century, penal philosophy evolved and prisoners began to be seen as patients in need of a cure. It was felt that if a prisoner was classified correctly and the right medicine given, they would be cured of their criminal ways. For young people between the age of 16 and 21, a system called Borstal was developed, named after the village where it was first started. Young people had to spend some time there and, depending on how well they did, they would be released after they were retrained and ready to live a crime-free life. It was felt that the habit of relapsing into crime was not impossible to solve—that the system would work and criminals would be cured. But once again disillusionment with the treatment system set in, as research studies established that it did not succeed and that sending people to prison did not 'cure' them. In fact, it almost made people worse.

A new philosophy started taking shape, which is now current in most West European countries. It is that, basically, prison is damaging to the individual, the family and the community. For one thing, its costs are high. These include the cost of the prison building, of the staff and of security, and of maintaining the prisoners.

The cost of a prisoner in England in 1995–1996 was £466 per week. In 2010 the cost of the prison system in England was about £3.1 billion. In the United States, the costs were $57 billion a year in 2003 and escalating. It is said that it costs as much to keep a prisoner in jail as at Harvard! Added to this are the social security costs of a family when the breadwinner has been taken away. There is a further cost from the damage caused by imprisonment because the ex-prisoner cannot easily find a job as a result of the stigma of a prison record and normally there is a family break-up.

In most West European countries, the government uses devices to reduce the numbers in prison, such as parole, waiting in a queue until a place is available, and suspended sentences for non-dangerous offenders so long as they observe good behaviour. Other alternative penalties are to deprive an offender of some aspect of liberty but to incorporate composite elements such as compensation and a commitment to self-improvement. Further, prisoners are helped to keep in touch with their families, learn useful skills in prisons and understand how to relate to the values of the outside world.

In India, imprisonment as a form of punishment was introduced by the British in 1773 and the more than 120-year-old Prisons Act of 1894 is still the law, subject to slight amendments. The National Human Rights Commission has been working for some time on a new bill called the Prison (Administration and Treatment of Prisoners) Bill, but this has so far not been enacted.

Imprisonment plays an important part in the crime policy of every country. In developing countries, imprisonment is at the heart of the penal system even though it is counter-productive and expensive to lock up people and make the state responsible for feeding them.

In some countries, people are imprisoned for very

minor offences, in others, for violent crimes. In India, the majority of those in prison are undertrials.

Overcrowding, lack of ventilation, inadequate nutrition, inaccessible medical care, etc. are all conditions that can worsen disease and speed the spread of infection. According to the World Health Organization, the level of TB in prisons is believed to be up to 100 times higher than that in the civilian population. In India, too, TB is the great killer. At the time of the enquiry into the death of Rajan Pillai in Tihar Jail, 76 per cent of deaths in prisons were attributed to tuberculosis. Even today, TB continues to be rampant in prisons. Often the disease is noticed and diagnosed after the point of no return. This is not only a denial of the right to medical care of a person in custody but also a source of exposure and infection to other unsuspecting inmates. The mandatory medical examination on admission of a person to prison is often a mere procedural formality or not conducted for days on end, as I observed in my report in 1997. Since then, medical facilities have been revamped and I believe that conditions have somewhat improved.

It is said that the penal system in the US is among the most severe. Though society in the US gives the impression of great liberality, the prisons of the country offer a spectacle of complete despotism. There has been a manifold increase in the number of prisoners since 1980. Violence is a widespread problem.

America calls itself the 'land of the free' but its investment in imprisonment has been massive, overtaking that in higher education. In fact, imprisonment is becoming big business, as prisons are being privatized.

Fortunately, in India, the number of prisoners per 100,000 of population is only about 30, of which the majority are undertrials. Most of them are male, poor, uneducated and unemployed and involved in petty offences. So if we act promptly, the problem is not without solution.

Women are also in prison, though in much smaller numbers. All over the world they are a tiny minority of those locked up and they are also often poor, exploited and abused. Sometimes they have killed a husband or a lover. Fathiyya in Egypt, known as 'the murderess', was such a woman. But the facts were that she was a poor miserable woman planting and harvesting with her own hands while her husband lounged about the house, smoking his water pipe. One day, she came back from the field and found him on top of her 9-year-old daughter. She struck him on the head with her hoe and got a life sentence.

Often, women are pregnant when they come to prison. In many countries, they are sent to outside hospitals to give birth. In England, a woman was kept handcuffed while she was giving birth so she could not even grip the bed rails during her labour pains. She also had to feed her baby with the handcuffs on.

In some countries, women are allowed to keep their babies, but in others they are not... It is a dilemma: a child growing up in prison or a child deprived of a mother's love and care?

The above-mentioned case of a woman giving birth while handcuffed is a clear violation of Article 10 of the United Nations Covenant on Civil and Political Rights, which says: 'All persons deprived of their liberty shall be treated with humanity and with respect for the inherent dignity of the human person.'

The same message is repeated in the European Convention on Human Rights, the African Charter on Human and People's Rights and the Inter-American Convention on Human Rights. The spirit of the United Nations Standard Minimum Rules for the treatment of prisoners and other such documents is that 'men come to prison as a punishment, not for punishment...' Yet these rules are repeatedly breached or else not adopted at all by some countries. Although in the short term we must humanize the jails, in the long term we must find a better way. As we have entered the third millennium, as well as the seventh decade of the United Nations Declaration on Human Rights, we need to ponder and ask ourselves: is there a good prison system, or is the idea of prison as such not a workable method for the majority of cases. I ask myself, how many people must the state lock up before it can call itself safe?

Should we not be thinking about alternative methods? Most studies of various prison systems indicate that it destroys people's lives and, despite heavy financial costs, fails to rehabilitate criminals. It is difficult for people to be trained for freedom when they are incarcerated.

Should there not be an all-round effort to spend more money and resources on violence prevention rather than on building stronger and better jails?

Here are some suggestions as alternatives to the prison system we have in India today:

1. For undertrials: In most cases bail, not jail, should be the answer, with or without conditions.

    It has been reported that about 70 per cent of the inmates in Central Jail, Tihar are involved in petty offences. They could all be released on bail. In fact, the Supreme Court has been recommending that all undertrials facing trial for over a year for certain petty offences be released. If this recommendation had been carried out, a large number of undertrials would have benefited and the jails would have become less crowded. The Supreme Court also directed the trial courts to 'speed up the trial of criminal cases to prevent the prosecution from becoming persecution of the persons arrayed in a criminal trial'. Further, the Chief Justice of the Supreme Court issued instructions to subordinate courts to grant bail to undertrials who could not furnish surety for bail bonds, provided they were otherwise entitled to it. The 78th Report of the Law Commission of India (1979) has also made some concrete recommendations in this regard.

    The Code of Criminal Procedure (Amendment) Act, 2005 provides that 'if the arrested person is accused of a bailable offence and he is indigent and

cannot furnish surety, the [Trial] Court shall release him on his execution of a bond without surety'. This ensures the release of such undertrials by the Trial Court itself without a statutory bail bond of a particular amount.
2. House arrest: Used with or without electronic devices in both pre- and post-sentence cases. (This is expensive and can be stigmatizing, as an anklet has to be worn.)
3. Victim–offender mediation schemes: If the offender admits guilt and the victim agrees, mediation in the presence of a competent person can be carried out, resulting in compensation for the victim, or some action to benefit society. The matter can then be closed.
4. Sentencing: A verbal sanction, warning, or reprimand can be issued, especially in the case of young offenders.
5. Conditional sentence: This would be based on not committing another crime for a specified period.
6. Suspended sentence: This would be based on not committing any other crime.
7. Fines for minor offences.
8. Financial penalties for financial and property offences: These would be congruent to the income of the offender.
9. Paying compensation to the victim.
10. Confiscation of licence or property: This can be applied to a serious driving offence or to people who have made substantial money in the drug trade.
11. Supervision by a social worker, probation officer

or other skilled person appointed by a competent authority: A supervisor helps a young offender to take better control of his/her life and be reintegrated into the community.
12. Certain restrictions on liberty of movement: This could involve the surrender of one's passport; restraining or enjoining a person from going to certain places or going out during certain hours, e.g. night curfew (especially for young offenders who are prone to consuming alcohol).
13. Open jails.
14. Various forms of parole: Releasing a prisoner for education or for looking after a parent or a family member who is ill, etc. depending on the individual problem and the prisoner's attitude.

   I made a suggestion in the report dealing with the Rajan Pillai Inquiry that persons above sixty-five years of age who are sick and infirm should be released on general parole so that they can go back to their family and be taken care of by their loved ones and die in peace. I also suggested that women prisoners be allowed to return to their family on parole at least one month before the time of giving birth since they require special care, support and attention, which they cannot get in prison.
15. Community service instead of imprisonment: The offender offers restitution to the whole community rather than to the individual victim. (The undertaking to work must be a voluntary choice in view of the

ILO Convention.) There could be part imprisonment and part community service. The community service could be environmental work; child care; care of old people; hospital work; manual work; construction or renovation of buildings, etc. This develops good working habits and a good relationship with public institutions.

The commentary to the UN Standard Minimum Rules for non-custodial measures (The Tokyo Rules) suggests: 'The work assigned to the offender should be socially useful and meaningful rather than pointless and should enhance the offender's skill as much as possible.'

Of course, in countries of high unemployment, this may cause some resentment.

■

For many years the Supreme Court of India has been asking the central and state governments to frame a uniform Jail Manual. A Model Prison Manual was framed in 2005 but is yet to be adopted by different states. The conditions prevailing in the various central jails, district jails, prisons for women and sub-jails accommodating about 3.8 lakh inmates have to be improved.

The directions of the Supreme Court of India, if properly implemented, could have a substantial effect on reducing the number of undertrial prisoners in jails and this would certainly result in better conditions.

The adoption of a system of plea bargaining and the introduction of a system of compensation for crime on the analogy of the criminal injuries compensation; a massive decriminalization of offences so that they can be dealt with as compoundable wrongs; promoting of NGOs for 'victim assistance and service' and for the protection of witnesses; and the evolution and implementation of appropriate training programmes for the members of the judiciary in human rights jurisprudence—all these have been suggested by the National Human Rights Commission. Many of these recommendations were also contained in the 154th Report of the Law Commission. They are being processed by government but, unfortunately, there does not appear to be any sense of urgency. Delay in implementing these reforms could well derail the criminal justice system.

The purpose of the criminal justice system is to protect society from serious violence and crimes of a sexual nature. The two basic requirements are recognition of the harm suffered by the victim and a protection from violence and abuse. Since it is necessary to protect people from murder, severe physical violence and sexual assault, in certain cases prison appears to be the only solution. But those in charge of the prisons where offenders are lodged must put in more effort to ensure that their violent reactions are contained and reduced rather than increased.

Society does need protection from organized crime gangs that threaten its stability. The rule of law has to be maintained and strict punishment enforced. But the major part of the resources available should be funnelled into violence prevention. Instead of spending more and more on expensive new jails and their maintenance, we must continually search for systems more relevant to our economic circumstances that do not consume all our resources, leaving nothing for crime prevention—or for services to help victims recover from the trauma of serious crime.

We should remove from prisons all those prisoners who pose no real danger to the public and are locked up, perhaps for years, for no sufficient reason. Often, their offences could have been dealt with in the community itself. As the elderly man in *No Full Stops in India* by Mark Tully says, 'The worst thing that has happened is that the police started coming into the village. In the old days the police never came—we used to sort out our quarrels ourselves or with the panchayat (village council). But nowadays people keep running to the court or the police station. They waste a lot of money and achieve nothing. The police are not just. They always side with the richer person, so no matter how much you offer them you can't beat someone with more money.'

Sanctions imposed by people who are personally concerned with an offence are much more effective than those imposed by a remote legal authority. What your neighbours and friends and family think of you is a very important factor in the way you see yourself. But it is important to give the right kind of sanction to the particular individual so that there is a useful outcome. Community service and compensation mean that something is paid back to society in general or to the victim in particular. It helps society to come together and helps to rebuild rather than cause more damage as happens when you lock someone away.

One is reminded of the anguished voice of the poet Oscar Wilde when he was in prison in Reading for an offence that is not an offence in Britain today:

> *I know not whether Laws be right,*
> *Or whether Laws be wrong,*
> *All that we know who lie in gaol*
> *Is that the wall is strong;*
> *And that each day is like a year,*
> *A year whose days are long.*
>
> *The vilest deeds like poison weeds*
> *Bloom well in prison air:*
> *It is only what is good in Man*
> *That wastes and withers there:*
> *Pale Anguish keeps the heavy gate,*
> *And the Warder is Despair.*

Prison is for reformation, not retribution. If we act on the principle of an eye for an eye, the world, as Gandhiji said, would be full of blind people.

The terrible suffering that is being inflicted on prisoners worldwide leaves one horrified. One cannot forget the words of Judith Ward, who served for eighteen years in Durham Prison before being cleared of charges against her. She was 25 years old when she was imprisoned for planting bombs that killed twelve people. She was given twelve life sentences. In 1992 her conviction was overturned and she was released, a victim of a gross miscarriage of justice. She recorded what she saw and had lived through. She said, 'Never could I forget, put it all behind me. I will never forget, more importantly—I will never let you forget.'

An institution devised for the eighteenth and nineteenth century has carried on, with only minor modifications, into the twentieth and twenty-first centuries. We must reflect on this and we must do something about this. Our emphasis should be on crime prevention, on the removal of illiteracy, poverty, inequality and unemployment, and on finding ways to make people proud of a just and democratic society.

Judicial Administration

The judicial administration system which prevails in India today has an essentially British background. The system of law that was originally adopted for India by the British administration was a mix of English common law and Indian customary law. As has been said, the former was tied up in technicalities and the latter contained 'a bewildering variety of ascertained, unascertained or unascertainable rules of doubtful origin and vague application'.

Lord Macaulay said: 'I believe that no country ever stood so much in need of a code of law as India, as I believe also that there never was a country in which the want might be so easily supplied. Our principle is simply this—uniformity when you can have it, diversity when you must have it; but, in all cases, certainty.'

Pioneering work was done by the 1st Law Commission in British India. It recommended that the personal law of the Hindus and the Muslims, which derived their authority from their respective religions, should not be codified. Without a perfect model, a 'consistent system of courts and laws' had to be evolved. The endeavour was to create a system which would be 'alike honourable to the English government and beneficial to the people of India'. Broadly, it was a system by which law and order could be preserved in British India and governance carried on smoothly, so that the efficient functioning of the rulers was not hampered.

Independence brought about a change in the psychology of India. The people of India gave to themselves a Constitution. Their status was altered from subjects in a dependency to citizens of a democratic republic. Prior to Independence, an English barrister of even one day's standing was held to be senior to an Indian advocate, no matter what his experience. This was one of the thousands of things that were changed. National consciousness grew, and this had an effect on social, economic and political life.

The Preamble to the Constitution states as aspirations for the country:

> JUSTICE, social, economic and political;
> LIBERTY of thought, expression, belief, faith and worship;
> EQUALITY of status and of opportunity; and...
> FRATERNITY assuring the dignity of the individual....

The nationalistic upsurge which had resulted in India securing independence gave the individual a distinct sense of pride. He also became conscious of the rights guaranteed to him by the Constitution. His right to liberty and to claim equality of status and opportunity, and social, economic and political justice quite often brought him into conflict with the state. This resulted in an increase in the number of persons who approached the courts for adjudication. Further, in the post-independence Constitution era, the central and state legislatures have passed many laws keeping in mind the well-being as well as the regulation of the activities of citizens. There has been an enormous legislative output of thousands of acts, ordinances, regulations, rules, etc.

The changed and more confident attitude of the citizen to approaching the courts, the advent of public interest litigation, the proliferation of laws, and the massive population explosion has resulted in the clogging of the courts. The infrastructure and strength of the courts have not kept pace with the demand and the result is a huge backlog. As of 1 April 2014, there were 64,330 matters pending in the Supreme Court alone. The pendency in the twenty-four different High Courts as of 31 December 2011 was 4,327,746. Of these, 3,395,674 were civil cases and 932,072 criminal cases. The subordinate courts are also overburdened with cases, with a total pendency of 26,986,307 as of 31 December 2011. And, to put it euphemistically, there does not appear to be any immediate hope of these arrears being cleared.

This brings to mind the oft-repeated adage, 'Justice delayed is justice denied.' Delayed justice is today perhaps the biggest bane of judicial administration in India. What use is a divorce decree when one is too old to remarry, or the return of a house when the owner is dead? In many of the High Courts of the country, civil appeals, writ petitions and even murder cases have been pending for hearing for many years.

In fact, as we've seen, criminal trials have sometimes been so tardy that persons who had either not been released on bail or could not furnish bail bonds had been in prison longer than the period for which they could have been imprisoned if convicted of a particular offence. When this was brought to the notice of the Supreme Court by way of public interest litigation, the court called for a report from the state governments and directed that the persons under trial be released forthwith.

With the length of pendency of cases not abating, and in fact increasing, it is necessary to examine how to keep the system in working order. In 1967 the Government of India appointed a committee to review the problem of arrears in the High Courts. In its report, the committee noted that one of the critical social problems was the acute congestion of cases, especially in the High Courts. There was gross delay in the disposal of pending files, leading to serious dissatisfaction in the public mind about the effectiveness of the court process for resolving the grievances of citizens.

In 1974 the Law Commission of India in its 58th Report observed that the strength and glory of our system of judicial administration rested solely on the confidence that it commanded from the community and that it should be the concern of all of us to devise, from time to time, legitimate, fair and effective ways and means of avoiding delays and the accumulation of arrears. Unfortunately, today, forty years later, it is clear that we are on the verge of this confidence being destroyed. The danger signals are apparent and we must act expeditiously.

What then are the multifaceted causes of delay? What are the methods that have been suggested and adopted to try and contain the system so that it does not burst at its seams? The factors to be considered are both procedural and human.

Once a case is filed in court, the first difficulty is that of serving a summons on either the party or the witnesses. Very often, the party interested in delaying the proceedings, e.g., a tenant in occupation, persuades the process-server to give a report that the summons could not be served. Next, when the case comes to court for hearing, counsel seek adjournments on flimsy grounds. They accept more work than they can handle and rush from court to court seeking postponements and not arguing effectively anywhere. Counsel for the opposite side, who have similar difficulties at other times, are more than willing to accommodate them. Weddings, festivities and funerals of not just close family members and friends but even acquaintances are given as grounds for seeking adjournment. The convenience of counsel should not be a reason for granting an adjournment, but the difficulty is that if counsel is not available, then there is no one to plead the case and this poses problems if finer questions of law have to be decided. Both these problems can be solved if process servers and counsel act in a more responsible way.

Another cause of delay is multifarious appeals from interlocutory orders, for example, those regarding the question of admissibility of evidence. Once the appeal is admitted, the proceedings in the trial court are stayed and this naturally results in delay.

Yet another cause is that arguments are verbose and repetitive. There is no limitation on the time taken for oral arguments. Since lawyers normally accept a daily fee rather than a consolidated fee there is no sense of urgency regarding disposal of the case. The quality of judges has gone down, while case complexities have increased. Further, the number of judges and the infrastructure of the delivery of justice have not been increased in proportion to the proliferating population and litigation.

As regards the number of judges: in the 120th Report of the Law Commission dated 31 July 1987, 'Manpower Planning in Judiciary: A Blueprint', it was suggested that the proportion of judge strength per million of population be increased.

According to this report, India at that time had only 10.5 judges per million people whereas England in 1973 had 50.9 judges per million people and the United States in 1982 had an average of 107 judges per million people. It was quite clear that the judge strength of 7,675 in India was 'grossly inadequate'. The commission was of the view that it was not possible to suggest a tenfold increase in view of the 'overall resource constraints', but stated that a fivefold increase should certainly be attempted within a span of five years.

The government's resistance to raising the ratio of judges is normally a question of finance. But, as was mentioned in the report, the nation 'pays far more exorbitant costs through the lack of adequate manpower planning than a reasonable investment in the judicial services'. The Law Commission was not able to precisely quantify the costs, but it indicated the headings:

(a) the total costs to the exchequer by stay orders of public revenue measures every decade;
(b) the human rights and dignity costs to people in custody assessed notionally in terms of the right to compensation for unauthorized detention at ₹50,000 per unit;
(c) the costs of litigation both to State and private parties;
(d) the overall costs of maintenance of law and order; and
(e) all-declining respect for the rule of law.

I emphasize and repeat the last head—an all-declining respect for the rule of law.

Looking at matters from 'the litigation rate' (i.e. the number of cases and petitions instituted per annum since Independence) or the 'rate of pendency', the commission also concluded that a conservative estimate would require a minimum increase of judge strength from 7,675 to 40,357, i.e. raising the ratio from 10.5 per million people to 50. It also mentioned that it was time to re-think whether expenditure on administration of justice should even be called 'non-plan expenditure'. The commission then recommended that by the year 2000 we should 'command' at least the ratio that the United States had in 1981, i.e. 107 judges per million of Indian population. Despite this report and many other reports since then, no effective steps have been taken to sufficiently increase the numbers of judges, whereas the population is increasing daily.

Another aspect of the matter is that even when the legally sanctioned judge strength is raised, the difficulty in making judicial appointments remains. From past history it appears that even the sanctioned posts are not filled when they fall vacant. A judge of the Punjab and Haryana High Court undertook an exercise in which he calculated judge days lost through not making judicial appointments on time i.e., as soon as the vacancy arose. It showed that a large chunk of the arrears would have disappeared if the judges had been put in position immediately a vacancy arose.

The date when a judge is due to retire is known and the process of appointing a judge in that vacancy should be initiated much earlier. In the Delhi High Court, when I was a judge (1978-1991), there was only one case where a successor judge was sworn in on the very day after the predecessor judge demitted office. It seems that even when the process is initiated in time, delays take place in large measure owing to what is called 'disputes as to the selection of the successor'.

It is pertinent to note that as of 15 August 2014,

the number of judges in the Supreme Court is thirty though the sanctioned strength is thirty-one. Seven of these appointments were made quite recently. And as of 1 April 2014 the total approved strength of judges in the High Courts is 906 but the actual working strength is only 649. The situation in the District and Subordinate judiciary appears to be no better—against a sanctioned strength of 17,715, more than 3,300 posts are vacant. Since vacancies and delays are inevitably correlated, it was recognized that a campaign mode approach for filling vacancies needed to be launched. Keeping this in mind, all the chief justices of the High Courts are constantly being requested to launch campaigns to reduce pendency and fill vacancies of judges.

Since judicial disposal is dependent on competent judicial personnel, the quality of the men and women in the judiciary must be of a high level. Consequently, the judicial career must be made sufficiently attractive for lawyers of high standing. The independence of judges is threatened not only by political pressure 'but by financial anxiety', as Lord Denning has observed. The High Court Judges (Salaries and Conditions of Service) Act, 1954 governs the service conditions of High Court judges, and it is modified from time to time. As of 1 April 2009, the prescribed salary of the chief justice of a High Court was ₹90,000 per month plus Dearness Allowance (D.A.) and other perks, and ₹80,000 plus D.A. and other perks for other High Court judges. Similarly, the Supreme Court Judges (Salaries and Conditions of Service) Act, 1958 (modified up to 1 April 2009), provides a salary of ₹1 lakh per month plus D.A. and perks to the Chief Justice of India, and ₹90,000 plus D.A. and perks for other Supreme Court judges. It remains to be seen if these changes will continue to attract the brightest at the Bar.

In 1958, in the 14th Report of the Law Commission, it was noticed that in the past, in the matter of appointment of High Court judges, the Chief Justice of the High Court had a preponderant voice. It then went on to note that the voice of the chief justice was not half as effective as it had been in the past.

Since then, the chief minister has had a hand, direct or indirect, in the matter of appointments to the High Court Bench. The inevitable result has been that the High Court appointments have not always been made on merit but often on extraneous considerations of community, caste, political affiliation and the grounds of personal likes and dislikes. This has encouraged canvassing, which is a distressing development. 'Formerly, a member of the Bar was invited to accept a judgeship and he considered it a great privilege and honour. Within a few years of Independence, however, the judgeship of a High Court seems to have become a post to be worked and canvassed for.'

Independent and efficient judges are an essential bulwark of freedom and linchpins in the effective administration of justice. The importance of an independent judiciary is much greater under a democratic constitution, as the court often has to decide not only the legality of actions of executive authorities but also those of legislative bodies when determining matters between the citizen and the state. Even in the UK, where there is no written constitution and Parliament is supreme, Sir Winston Churchill said:

> The principle of complete independence of the judiciary from the executive is the foundation of many things in our island life. The Judge has not only to do justice between man and man. He also—and this is one of the most important functions considered incomprehensible in some large parts of the world—has to do justice between the citizens and the State. He has to ensure that the administration conforms with the law, and to adjudicate upon the legality of the exercise by the executive of its powers...
>
> The service rendered by Judges demands the highest qualities of learning, training, and character. These qualities are not to be measured in terms of pounds, shillings and pence according to the quantity of work done. A form of life and conduct far more severe and restricted than that of ordinary people is required from Judges, and though unwritten, has been most strictly observed. They are at once privileged and restricted. They have to present a continuous aspect of dignity and conduct.

Our Supreme Court had occasion to dilate on these matters in *S. P. Gupta and Others vs Union of India and Others*, in what has now come to be known as the First Judges' Case. The chief justice had this to say:

In securing and promoting the resolution of disputes in a legal forum in accordance with established legal procedure, the administration of justice ensures a peaceful and orderly progress by a people through constitutional methods towards the realization of their aspirations. And if it is to rule their minds and hearts, the administration of justice must enjoy their confidence. Public confidence in the administration of justice is imperative to its effectiveness, because ultimately the ready acceptance of a judicial verdict alone gives relevance to the judicial system. While the administration of justice draws its legal sanction from the Constitution, its credibility rests in the faith of the people. Indispensable to that faith is the independence of the judiciary. An independent and impartial judiciary supplies the reason for the judicial institution, it also gives character and content to the constitutional milieu.

India's statesmen, political leaders, eminent jurists and representatives of a broad cross-section of our national life were engaged for about three years in forging a Constitution worthy of India's greatness. In the fashioning of the provisions relating to the judiciary, the greatest importance was attached to securing the independence of the Judges, and throughout the Constituent Assembly debates the most vigorous emphasis was laid on that principle. The judiciary in British India had by and large, for a century of British rule, enjoyed the respect and confidence of the people for its high reputation of independence and impartiality.

Nonetheless, the framers of the Constitution took great pains to ensure that an even better and more effective judicial structure was incorporated in the Constitution, one which would meet the highest expectations of judicial independence. In a land and among a people whose ancient values stemmed from truth as a reality, culminating in the adoption of a national emblem confirming that creed, they could have done no less.

But finally it was held in that case that under Article 217(1) of the Constitution, it was the executive power of the President of India to appoint a judge of a High Court and that this power was conditioned only by an obligation to consult the Chief Justice of India, the Governor of the State, and, in the case of a judge other than the chief justice, the Chief Justice of the High Court. However, consultation did not mean concurrence and as such the views expressed by the chief justice and others were not binding on the Government of India, who had the ultimate power of making the appointment.

Since government is the largest single litigant, there was a body of opinion that felt that the government was in a position to destroy the independence of the judiciary by appointing and transferring persons of their choice, overruling the recommendations of the High Court chief justices and the Chief Justice of India. Thus, the judiciary itself would become politicized.

In 1993, a nine-judge bench reconsidered the decision in *S. P. Gupta and Others vs Union of India and Others* in

Supreme Court Advocates-on-Record Association vs Union of India. (This is popularly known as the Second Judges' Case.) The majority view was that in the matter of appointments and transfers of High Court and Supreme Court judges the opinion of the Chief Justice of India had primacy. Thereafter, the Supreme Court adopted the collegium system, under which appointments and transfers of judges were to be decided by a forum of the Chief Justice of India and the two senior-most judges of the Supreme Court, later changed to four. This position was clarified in Reference No. 1 of 1998, *In Re: Presidential Reference*, known as the Third Judges' Case.

However, it is pertinent to point out that there is no mention of such a system in the Constitution. Article 124(2) of the Constitution states that the appointments of Supreme Court judges are to be made by the president after consultation with such judges of the Supreme Court and High Courts as the president may deem necessary. The Chief Justice of India is to be consulted on all appointments except his own. In the case of High Court judges, the appointment is made under Article 217(1) as indicated earlier.

Unfortunately, the collegium system too has not worked as well as expected. One of the main problems with it is a total lack of transparency and no specified criteria. Justice Ruma Pal, a former judge of the Supreme Court, has referred to this process of recommendation for appointment as 'one of the best kept secrets in the country'. There are serious questions as to whether the pendulum has swung too far the other way. Many suggestions were made to broad base judicial appointments and introduce accountability and transparency.

This issue was examined, at the behest of the NDA government, by the National Commission to Review the Working of the Constitution, chaired by Justice M.N. Venkatachaliah, a former Chief Justice of India. The report was submitted in 2002 and the suggestion made in this regard for appointment of judges of the Supreme Court was for a five-member commission. This would comprise the Chief Justice of India (chairman); two of the senior-most judges of the Supreme Court; the Union Minister for Law and Justice; and one eminent person nominated by the president in consultation with the Chief Justice of India.

Subsequently, a bill to do away with the collegium system and to set up a Judicial Appointments Commission (JAC) was introduced by the UPA government in the Rajya Sabha in August 2013. The bill sought to set up a six-member commission consisting of the Chief Justice of India (chairperson), the two senior-most judges of the Supreme Court, the law minister and two eminent persons. The committee to nominate these two eminent persons would consist of the Prime Minister of India, the Chief Justice of India and the Leader of the Opposition in the Lok Sabha. The Secretary (Justice) in the Law Ministry (not a member of the commission) would act as the convener. This was an attempt to hold a balance between the judiciary and the executive.

The Minister of Law and Justice of the new NDA government (2014), however, expressed some reservations about this bill and wanted to rework it. He invited distinguished senior advocates, jurists and some retired judges for a discussion. I was not one of the invitees, but this did not prevent me from thinking about the bill and its implications for the independence of the judiciary, which is of paramount importance.

It appeared to me that in order to preserve the independence of the judiciary, the dominant voice should be that of the judiciary. We clearly should not go back to the pre-1993 position.

The JAC Bill provided for a six-member commission, an even number that that could get deadlocked. I would have favoured an odd number, that is, a seven-member commission, which would include the three senior-most judges of the Supreme Court, rather than two, as suggested in the bill. With regard to the committee to nominate two eminent persons to the JAC, I would have clarified that if there is no Leader of the Opposition in the Lok Sabha, then the leader of the largest single party should take his place. Further, one of the two eminent persons should be a distinguished jurist and the other a member of civil society. The JAC should not be an ad hoc body but a permanent body and its composition should be ensured by a constitutional amendment and not by an ordinary statute. The recommendations of the JAC should be binding, and only altered if there are strong reasons, recorded in writing and made public. In order

Talking of Justice

to institutionalize the system, certain criteria regarding competence, integrity, age, etc. should be indicated.

I was hopeful that something of this kind would work better than the collegium system. No model is ever perfect, and the people who man it make all the difference, but it is important that they should be aware that their reasons, recorded in writing, can be seen by the public at large.

As I was thinking about these matters and wondering what changes would be introduced in the JAC Bill, suddenly, on 13 August 2014, the 121st Constitution Amendment Bill and a new bill entitled the National Judicial Appointments Commission Bill, 2014 (NJAC) were introduced and passed in the Lok Sabha. This new bill also provided for a six-member commission and its main features were more or less the same as those of the earlier bill of 2013. There were, however, two new items in the bill, which the Congress Party wanted removed. In order to get the bills passed in the Rajya Sabha the next day, the government agreed to drop one of these contested clauses, but it did not change the new veto power introduced in the bill. According to this clause, if two members of the six-member commission did not agree to an appointment, they could veto it.

The great haste in introducing and getting these two very important bills passed in Parliament, without any substantial discussion and without their even being considered by a select committee is surprising when one considers that they will not be effective till the

Constitution Amendment Bill has been ratified by half the states, which may take a few months, before it gets the president's assent.

Whether the NJAC Act will eventually pass the test of preserving the independence of the judiciary is uncertain. There are clearly two views on the matter. But the independence of the judiciary is a basic feature of the Constitution and this six-member commission, where the judiciary is not paramount, is in danger of resulting in a Fourth Judges' Case and of being struck down by the Supreme Court.

■

The pattern of litigation has changed over the years. Conventional civil litigation arose primarily from disputes pertaining to partition of property, money claims, mortgage suits, adoptions etc. Since the commencement of the Constitution and the concomitant change in the concept of state functions with regard to both control over economic activity and as well as socio-economic well-being, there has been a tremendous increase in the number of Acts passed by Parliament and the state legislatures. These are normally accompanied by delegated legislative powers, resulting in rules, regulations and by-laws, which are often loosely drafted. Consequently, they are challenged in courts, and this gives rise to complicated questions of the validity and the permissible limits of delegated legislation.

Pleas regarding the infringement of fundamental rights guaranteed by the Constitution also result in a very large number of cases in which rules, notifications, circulars and even executive orders are challenged. Since the concept of 'the state' in Article 12 of the Constitution has been held to include public sector corporations etc., the number of cases has multiplied by leaps and bounds. The result is that today a large portion of litigation in courts, including writ petitions, consists of cases to which the government is a party.

The Law Commission in its 100th Report had occasion to examine this matter. It observed that the hardship caused to parties in such litigation, as also the delay experienced in its disposal, is largely due to certain defects in the law and in the administrative apparatus: overzealous government departments or officers, not properly oriented or guided, often miss the point of the matter and unknowingly contribute to a sizeable mass of avoidable litigation against the government. A noticeable feature of this litigation is that the High Courts and the Supreme Court are approached not only for redress regarding governmental acts that constitute an infringement of legal rights but also for redress regarding governmental acts that constitute instances of maladministration.

Taking note of this background, the Law Commission was of the opinion that there was a need for evolving some mechanism whereby the pressure on the courts could be relieved and the legal grievances of citizens redressed quickly and cheaply. It felt that this type of litigation would keep increasing over the years, initiated either by individuals or by public spirited bodies under the category of public interest litigation. Since it is common experience that, once litigation commences, there is considerable expense of time, money and labour for all parties, the commission felt that, as far as possible, the administrative apparatus should be so geared that the possibility of unnecessary litigation against the government would be avoided. With this end in view, the commission envisaged the creation of the office of a litigation ombudsman to whom a prospective litigant could (but was not obliged to) have recourse for the redress of his grievances of a justiciable character. The litigation ombudsman, after examining a matter, would have the power to make a recommendation with respect to any decision, act or omission of the government or its officer. Since people do not like to resort to litigation unless they have no choice, the litigation ombudsman could thus help relieve the congestion in the higher courts. But nothing has come of this suggestion.

In order to secure greater disposal of cases, the Law Commission, in its 99th Report, considered whether the time taken in oral arguments should be reduced so as to make it possible for the higher courts to hear a larger number of cases on each working day. The idea was that there should be speedy disposal, including reasonably swift and improved judgments.

After noting the sharp differences of views expressed by those in favour of some time limit and those strongly opposed to any change, a middle view emerged that recognized a need to place some reasonable limit on oral arguments but did not favour any hard and fast mathematical limit. With regard to written arguments, it was contended that they should not be allowed; that judges should make their own notes and that they should firmly but courteously prevent repetition in court.

On the question of the maximum time for oral arguments, the commission recommended that the matter be left to the judge concerned who, after consulting counsel, and keeping in mind various factors, such as the complexity of the case, the nature of the issues, the volume and character of evidence etc. could determine this. A statement of case/appeal properly prepared by counsel should be filed in court, and if counsel considered it necessary, they could be permitted to file written briefs (of reasonable length) which naturally would be more elaborate than the statement of case/appeal.

In regard to cases involving constitutional questions, the practice of filing briefs containing written factual material should be encouraged, wherever factual material formed the background of the case. The commission felt that so-called 'Brandeis briefs' would be very useful in constitutional adjudication as, in addition to affidavits filed on behalf of the parties, they contain facts relevant for constitutional adjudication (such as those derived from, say, medical or sociological research) as well as extracts from published reports of committees and commissions.

It further recommended that the system of providing law clerks attached to particular judges should be fully tried out. Law clerks would assist the judges in legal research by providing inputs and thereby assist indirectly in the writing of judgments. According to me, this was a step in the right direction. However, it not clear how effective this system has been as not all judges are always assigned law clerks—and their calibre is very variable.

Another method suggested for reducing delays was to decentralize the administration of justice and to have specialized tribunals to deal with various kinds of litigation arising from different enactments. Since the rigid procedures of the court system do not have to be followed by such tribunals, they would also help in quick disposal; further, there is more likely to be consistency in the decisions.

The Income Tax Appellate Tribunals and the Sales Tax Appellate Tribunals, which were established many years ago, have been effective, as have the Customs, Excise and Gold Control Tribunals that were established to deal with those matters. Labour Courts and Industrial Tribunals are also functioning. The Central and Regional Administrative Tribunals were established to deal with the service matters of civil servants. The number of writ petitions pending in the High Courts pertaining to such matters were very numerous, so these tribunals helped relieve, to some extent, the workload of the courts.

In India, judges do not sit in particular divisions (i.e. by subject), but do various types of work, as assigned by the chief justice, either singly or otherwise, and for certain periods of time. I am of the view that classification of work is essential so that there can be quicker, more consistent, and more effective disposal. A judge should be assigned, wherever possible, the kind of work at which he excels. If a bench is constituted for a particular class of cases, it should be allowed to function for a reasonable length of time.

Another suggestion that has been made at various times and with which I wholeheartedly agree is that each court should make use of its most experienced and competent judges to deal with the admission of cases. This is because, if matters are examined carefully at the admission stage and only the really deserving cases are admitted, there will be a great saving in the courts' time, as statistics indicate that 70 per cent to 80 per cent of the cases admitted are eventually dismissed at the time of final hearing.

Even after a matter has been heard, sometimes the judgment of the court is not pronounced for many months. This is partly due to the heavy workload, prolix arguments and indifferent assistance by counsel, and partly due to the desire to write an erudite judgment. These judgments are usually lengthy and often also deal with matters not directly at issue. But delay in the writing of judgments, quite apart from leading to poor disposal figures, sometimes leads to injustice as well, since judges—even with the help of their notes—cannot fully recall the issues and arguments of a case before them months (or even years) earlier.

A committee of three High Court chief justices which was set up in pursuance of a resolution of the Chief

Justices' Conference, 1983 in order to study the problem of arrears in High Courts and to suggest reforms made the following recommendation on this aspect:

> The judgments should be short, lucid and confined to the points arising in the case. The judges are neither equipped nor qualified to be philosophers or preachers. They should not consider themselves as Judicial Popes. The Courts have no right to decline jurisdiction, which is conferred on them or to usurp that which is not given.

This committee made various other suggestions pertaining to jurisdiction and procedure, recording of evidence, dictating judgments in open court, grouping and listing of appeals, and use of computer technology.

It also discussed the inadequacy of the court staff and paucity of accommodation, which contributed in no small measure to the accumulation of arrears.

The increase in staff in the High Courts has been less than proportionate to the increase in the case load, and consequently notices, etc., are not issued expeditiously, which results in further delays. Financial constraints have been the main reason given by the government for not sanctioning additional staff and accommodation.

The Supreme Court's docket has also become unmanageable. This explosion of litigation in the apex court is partly due to public interest litigation and the expansion of the doctrine of locus standi ever since the court permitted postcards, letters, telegrams and even newspaper articles to be treated as writ petitions. Often, these writs have been given priority over the normal work of the court. This has naturally resulted in further arrears and loss of the hope of speedy disposal to the litigant who is waiting in the queue. The process of public interest litigation has now been somewhat streamlined.

The other reason for the docket being overtaxed is the large number of special leave petitions that are filed in the Supreme Court and which are heard and dealt with in open court. But the problem is becoming so acute that a solution has to be found or else there will be absolutely no time for study and reflection, which are prerequisites for sound decision-making and judgment.

Consequent to the backlog, one of the questions being debated is the proper role of the Supreme Court. Should it be a court primarily for upholding and interpreting the Constitution or should it be required to deal also with ordinary judicial business like labour disputes, landlord and tenant matters, custody of children, etc. In this context there has been some discussion about splitting the functions of the Supreme Court into a Constitutional Court and an Appellate Court. There have been similar suggestions to also split the state High Courts into two tiers. This would definitely help reduce the number of appeals, as the High Court will be the last court of appeal in most cases.

As observed by a judge of the Supreme Court: 'I have no doubt that if a right of appeal were provided from the judgment of the highest court, a number of its decisions would be reversed in appeal. The Supreme

Court, it has been said, is not final because it is infallible; it is infallible because it is final.'

With regard to the avoidance of multiple appeals, a quotation from Paton's *Textbook of Jurisprudence* (1973) is relevant:

> To create a right of one appeal is reasonable, to allow three courts in ascending hierarchy to decide a matter seems an excess of caution, but to have a hierarchy of four or more courts seems to be based only on a decision to aid the legal profession.

There is a group of people who feel that the present system of justice is colonial and 'alien to our genius', and is the cause of all the existing ills, including the delays in disposal and the huge backlog. In a literal sense, the present system may be alien as it is a version of the British system, modified to suit Indian conditions. But it is important to remember, as observed by Justice H. R. Khanna, that this very system ensured, before 1947, that most criminal cases in the Magistrates' Courts were disposed of within four months, that a murder trial in the court of Sessions normally took about two months after the committal procedure (except in exceptional cases), and that most civil cases were disposed of within one year. Criminal appeals were disposed of within a couple of months and civil appeals remained pending for less than a year. It is, therefore, not correct to say that this system itself is the stumbling block in providing speedy administration of justice. The system is dependent on its inputs and, as discussed earlier, the inputs have not been adequate.

Can we revert to the earlier, historic, traditional pattern of Indian judicial administration? It would appear not. The success of the ancient system lay in its popular courts, which were founded on community or caste. A village was sufficient unto itself and managed its own affairs, the sustaining force being the respect which people had for customary law. There was no centralization then as there is now owing to the growth of a strong centralized system of government. The law administered today is not customary law. Thousands of statutes, regulations, etc., control, sometimes to the minutest detail, the lives and activities of every citizen of India. The Fundamental Rights of the people, as also the Directive Principles of State Policy, which have been enshrined in our Constitution, require for their realization an independent judiciary, a competent Bar and well defined rules of procedure.

The way to reform lies not in abandoning the present system but in trying to remove the defects that have crept in so that it meets our requirements for the present and the future. As society advances, it needs to alter from time to time the system which governs its functioning. A system of judicial administration is a matter of slow growth and its advance is moulded by contemporary conditions and existing social structures.

Though it is not possible in the conditions which prevail today to do away with professional courts, yet, to a limited extent, it is possible to utilize some of the simple features of the judicial administration of the past, like Nyaya Panchayats (Village Courts).

Writing in the *Harijan* in 1935, Mahatma Gandhi said that justice in British courts was an expensive luxury. He said that it was often 'the longest purse that wins', and he suggested that one should agree with one's adversary quickly so that litigation could be avoided. He felt that conciliation was the answer. One measure enacted for reducing litigation has been mediation at the grass-roots level. Lok Adalats (People's Courts) have been set up and a large number of compensation cases settled. More recently, the enactment of the Gram Nyayalayas Act, 2008, has helped to improve access to justice for the marginalized.

As already observed, the proper administration of justice is dependent foremost on a fearless and honest judiciary. Justice Jackson said that judges are more often bribed by their ambitions and loyalty than by money. Many believe that the decision of the five-person bench of the Supreme Court in the so called 'Habeas Corpus' case during the Emergency, with only Justice H.R. Khanna dissenting, is a case in point here.

As Lord Devlin observed: 'Judges are not now, neither have they been in the past, much better or much worse than other public servants.' He further said: 'We can now say that the British Judges are universally known to be above bribery, we can also say the same of any Minister of the Crown and any of the higher civil servants.' The moral is 'that integrity comes haltingly into public life and that without watchfulness it may slip away'.

The distinguished lawyer H. M. Seervai, delivering the Chimanlal Setalvad Lectures in 1970, agreed wholeheartedly with Lord Devlin on the close connection between integrity in public life and in the judiciary. If standards of integrity are lowered, or brought into conformity with standards of a society which treats corruption in public life as part of its way of life, the basis of an incorruptible higher judiciary is vitiated. No constitutional safeguards can secure an incorruptible judiciary unless the men who appoint judges, and the men who are appointed judges, are imbued with the high standards of public administration on which those safeguards rest.

Mr Seervai also commented that the traditions in India of an incorruptible higher judiciary are so high and the departure from those traditions so rare that we are apt to take such a judiciary for granted. But then, he continued, we must look ahead twenty or thirty years from now. What are the traditions in which the young lawyer joining the Bar today is being brought up? Will he accept the high traditions of public life and administration if the community at large rejects them, not by words but by deeds? He went on to say that, although unpleasant, it is necessary to remind ordinary citizens that an incorruptible judiciary, which they may take for granted and to which they confidently turn for the protection of their rights, whether against the state or against individuals, cannot survive if they do not demand and secure integrity in public life.

It is more than forty years since he spoke these words.

A time of crisis is indeed upon us and 'watchfulness' is the need of the hour.

■

One final point: the desirability of separating the investigative arm of the police from that portion of the police that deals with general problems of law and order has been mentioned in the 77th Report of the Law Commission. An investigating agency burdened with other duties is not able to ensure prompt and efficient investigation of crime nor can it be of assistance in the speedy disposal of court cases and the prevention of miscarriages of justice. As Justice Khanna has observed, wrongful acquittals are as undesirable as wrongful convictions. Both shake the confidence of the people in the administration of justice. Moreover, wrongful acquittals provide encouragement to criminals and the enemies of society. Whatever be the reason for the failure of the prosecution to secure proper convictions—whether it is the patronage of local politicians protecting the accused or lack of proper investigation by the police or the police being engaged in other work so that they cannot prosecute cases in court expeditiously—it erodes the people's confidence in the capacity of the courts to get at the truth and do justice. Once an impression becomes prevalent that culprits cannot be convicted and punished in a court of law, victims and their relatives start taking recourse to extra-legal methods for settling scores. Such a situation leads naturally to a state of chaos and anarchy.

Something has to be done about this urgently, for in the words of Judge Curtis Raleigh: 'The law should not be seen to sit by limply, while those who defy it go free and those who seek its protection lose hope.'

You're Criminal if Gay

My name is Leila Seth. I am 83 years old. I have been in a long and happy marriage of more than sixty years with my husband Premo, and am the mother of three children. The eldest, Vikram, is a writer. The second, Shantum, is a Buddhist teacher. The third, Aradhana, is an artist and filmmaker. I love them all. My husband and I have brought them up with the values we were brought up with—honesty, courage, and sympathy for others. We know that they are hardworking and affectionate people who are trying to do some good in the world.

But our eldest, Vikram, is now a criminal, an unapprehended felon. This is because, like many millions of other Indians, he is gay; and, last month, two judges of the Supreme Court overturned the judgment of two judges of the Delhi High Court that, four years ago, decriminalized homosexuality. Now, once again, if Vikram falls in love with another man, he will be committing a crime punishable by imprisonment for life if he expresses his love physically. The Supreme Court judgment means that he would have to be celibate for the rest of his life or else leave the country where he was born, to which he belongs, and which he loves more than any other.

I myself have been a judge for more than fourteen years—first as a judge of the Delhi High Court, then as Chief Justice of the Himachal Pradesh High Court. Later, I served as a member of the Law Commission as well as the Justice J. S. Verma Committee, which resulted in the Criminal Law (Amendment) Act, 2013 being passed. I have great respect for legal proprieties in general, and would not normally comment on a judgment, but I am making an exception in this case.

I read the judgment of the Delhi High Court when it came out four years ago. It was a model of learning, humanity, and application of Indian constitutional principles. It was well crafted, and its reasoning clearly set out. It decided that Section 377 of the Indian Penal Code infringed Article 14 of the Constitution, which deals with the fundamental right to equality. It infringed Article 15, which deals with the fundamental right to non-discrimination. And it infringed Article 21, which covers the fundamental right to life and liberty, including privacy and dignity. The judgment of the High Court 'read down' Section 377 in order to decriminalize private, adult, consensual sexual acts.

The government found no fault with the judgment and did not appeal. However, a number of people who had no real standing in the matter did challenge it. Two judges of the Supreme Court heard the appeal in early 2012. Then, twenty-one months later, and on the very morning of the retirement of one of them, the judgment was finally pronounced. The Delhi High Court judgment was set aside, Section 377 was reinstated in full, and even private, adult, consensual sexual acts other than the one considered 'natural' were criminalized again.

As the mother of my elder son, I was extremely upset. But as a lawyer and a former judge, I decided to reserve my views till I had read the judgment. When I read it, it would be true to say that I found it difficult to follow its logic.

A host of academics and lawyers have critiqued the judgment in great detail, including the nonaddressal of the Article 15 argument, and have found it wanting in many respects. I do not intend to repeat those criticisms. However, I should point out that both learning and science get rather short shrift. Instead of welcoming cogent arguments from jurisprudence outside India, which is accepted practice in cases of fundamental rights, the judgment specifically dismisses them as being irrelevant.

Further, rather than following medical, biological, and psychological evidence, which shows that homosexuality is a completely natural condition, part of a range not only of human sexuality but of the sexuality of almost every animal species we know, the judgment continues to talk in terms of 'unnatural' acts, even as it says that it would be difficult to list them.

But what has pained me and is more harmful is the spirit of the judgment. The interpretation of law is untempered by any sympathy for the suffering of others.

The voluminous accounts of rape, torture, extortion

and harassment suffered by gay and transgender people as a result of this law do not appear to have moved the court. Nor does the court appear concerned about the parents of such people, who stated before the court that the law induced in their children deep fear, profound self-doubt, and the inability to peacefully enjoy family life. I know this to be true from personal experience. The judgment fails to appreciate the stigma that is attached to persons and families because of this criminalization.

The judgment claimed that the fact that a minuscule fraction of the country's population was gay or transgender could not be considered a sound basis for reading down Section 377. In fact, the numbers are not small. If only 5 per cent of India's more than a billion people are gay, which is probably an underestimate, it would be more than 50 million people, a population as large as that of Rajasthan or Karnataka or France or England. But even if only a very few people were in fact threatened, the Supreme Court could not abdicate its responsibilities to protect their fundamental rights, or shuffle them off to Parliament. It would be like saying that the Parsi community could be legitimately imprisoned or deported at Parliament's will because they number only a few tens of thousands. The reasoning in the judgment that justice based on fundamental rights can only be granted if a large number of people are affected is constitutionally immoral and inhumane.

The judgment has treated people with a different sexual orientation as if they are people of a lesser value.

What makes life meaningful is love. The right that

makes us human is the right to love. To criminalize the expression of that right is profoundly cruel and inhumane. To acquiesce in such criminalization or, worse, to recriminalize it is to display the very opposite of compassion. To show exaggerated deference to a majoritarian Parliament when the matter is one of fundamental rights is to display judicial pusillanimity, for there is no doubt that in the constitutional scheme it is the judiciary that is the ultimate interpreter.

A review petition is now up for hearing before one of the two original judges plus another, who will replace the now retired Justice G. S. Singhvi. It will be heard in chambers. No lawyers will be present.

I began by saying that Premo and I had brought up our children to believe in certain values. I did not mention some others that we have also sought to inculcate in them: to open their hearts and minds; to admit their errors frankly, however hard this may be; to abjure cruelty; and to repair in a willing spirit any unjust damage they have done to others.

When this article was first published on 26 January 2014, the review petition was pending. A few days later, this petition was dismissed without comment.

Subsequently, however, a curative petition has been filed and the Supreme Court has ordered it to be heard for admission in open court before a bench of five judges. This is the last judicial option available.

Acknowledgements

Writing is a lonely exercise, but a book needs help from others. This came my way mainly from friends. Some read the whole manuscript and critiqued it; others made suggestions on individual essays or helped with accessing material and updates. The names that come to my mind are: A.K Shiv Kumar, Frederika Meijer, Kiran Datar, Maja Daruwalla, Pavan Sharma, Poonam Mutreja, Shanti Verma, Soli Sorabjee and Syeda Hameed. There may be others whom I have forgotten as memory fades. But I thank them all.

A special word of thanks to Pujitha Krishnan, my editor at Aleph Book Company, who painstakingly updated the facts, helped reorganize and sequence the material and read the manuscript with me. And a big hug to my home editor and son, Vikram Seth, who kept his own writing in abeyance while he meticulously corrected the punctuation, words and grammar, and made suggestions regarding the content, even though he is not a lawyer.

I would also like to thank Bena Sareen, who has designed the unusual and attractive book jacket, and Premo Seth, my husband, for his endless patience and encouragement.

Chapter Notes

GENDER SENSITIZATION OF THE JUDICIARY
Adapted from *The World of Gender Justice,* Bhandare, M. C. (Ed.) 1999.
29 *State of Punjab:* AIR (1996) SC 1393.
33 *Vishakha vs State of Rajasthan:* AIR (1997) SC 3011.

SOCIAL ACTION LITIGATION
Adapted from talk given at a conference on The Constitution of South Africa from a Gender Perspective, January 1995.
38 **He held that Article 39A:** *M. H. Hoskot vs State of Maharashtra,* AIR (1978) SC 1548.
38 **This decision is remarkable:** The Directive Principles promote the concept of a welfare state and, in terms of Article 37 of the Indian Constitution, are 'fundamental in the governance of the country'. It is the duty of the state 'to apply these principles in making laws'.
38 *Hussainara Khatoon and Others:* AIR (1979) SC 1360 and 1369.
40 **'reasonable, fair and just':** The dynamic decision of *Maneka Gandhi vs Union of India,* (AIR (1978) SC 597) was relied on to support the court's reasoning in respect of this principle.
40 *Municipal Council, Ratlam:* AIR (1980) SC 1622.
40 *People's Union for Democratic Rights:* AIR (1982) SC 1473.
44 **The court viewed this letter:** AIR (1983) SC 378.
46 *Upendra Baxi and Others:* (1983) 2 SCC 308 and (1986) 4 SCC 106.

47 **Treated as a writ petition:** WP No. 2526 of 1982.
48 ***Joint Women's Programme:*** AIR (1987) SC 2060.
48 **The letter was registered:** AIR (1989) SC 1783.
49 **In 1990, Gaurav Jain:** AIR (1990) SC 292.
49 **Problems relating to prostitution:** AIR (1990) SC 1412.
51 **However, the court observed:** The Suppression of Immoral Traffic in Women and Girls Act, 1956, subsequently renamed the Immoral Traffic (Prevention) Act, is aimed at eradicating the evils of prostitution and providing prostitutes with an opportunity to become respectable members of society. The court also referred, in this regard, to provisions of the Indian Penal Code, the Juvenile Justice Act and the Indian Constitution.
52 ***Delhi Domestic Working Women's Forum:*** Judgment of 19 October 1994, WP No. 362 of 1993.
56 **In relation to the status:** The 73rd and 74th Amendments.
57 **In this regard:** WP No. 7059 of 1994.

WOMEN'S RIGHTS
Combined and adapted from the keynote address at the Seminar on Gender Issues, March 2000 and a talk given at the Salzburg Seminar, August 2000.
63 ***Mohammed Ahmed Khan:*** AIR (1985) SC 945.
69 **And while justice has eluded:** The state filed an appeal against the acquittal in the High Court. According to reports, until 2007, there had been only one hearing and two of the alleged accused had died.

A UNIFORM CIVIL CODE TOWARDS GENDER JUSTICE
Adapted from a talk given on the occasion of the Centenary Memorial Lecture for Renuka Ray, April 2005.
75 **Legal Aid Cell of AGHS:** In 1980 Asma Jahangir and three others set up the first all-female law firm in Pakistan called AGHS. Subsequently, in 1986, AGHS set up the first legal aid centre in Pakistan.

Chapter Notes

79 **Kerala had abolished:** The Kerala Joint Hindu Family System (Abolition) Act, 1975.
79 **Andhra Pradesh:** Hindu Succession (Andhra Pradesh Amendment) Act, 1986.
79 **Tamil Nadu:** Hindu Succession (Tamil Nadu Amendment) Act, 1989.
79 **Maharashtra:** Hindu Succession (Maharashtra Amendment) Act, 1994.
79 **Karnataka:** Hindu Succession (Karnataka Amendment) Act, 1994.
85 **the liberty of abandoning:** However, in February 2014, the Supreme Court ruled that personal law cannot stop Muslims and other religious minority members from adopting children under the secular law, i.e. the Juvenile Justice (Care and Protection of Children) Act, 2000. This is a judicious step towards a Uniform Civil Code enjoined by the Directive Principles in the Constitution.

CHILDREN'S RIGHTS

Adapted from 'Protecting Human Rights of Children and Women Warrant Top Priority'—a talk given at the Salzburg Seminar, International Legal Perspectives on Human Rights, August 2001.
99 *M.C. Mehta:* AIR (1991) SC 417.
100 **right to a dignified life:** *Unni Krishnan J.P. and Others vs State of Andhra Pradesh and Others,* AIR (1993) SC 2178.
101 *Lalima Gupta and Others:* AIR (1993) Himachal Pradesh 11.

THE GIRL CHILD

Combined and adapted from the Durgabai Deshmukh Memorial Lecture, 1997 and a talk on the occasion of the Golden Jubilee of India International Centre, 2012.
110 **The study found that:** The 2011 Census figures seem to suggest a connection between affluence and the sex ratio. A case

in point is Gurgaon in Haryana, which was one unit in the 2001 census, and which has been split into Gurgaon and Mewat in the 2011 census. Gurgaon, clearly the more economically advanced, modern and urbanized district, has a much lower child sex ratio of 826 females per 1,000 males as compared to Mewat with a CSR of 903.

115 **Since 1951:** Over the four decades from 1951 to 1991, the female literacy rate went up about fivefold from 8.86 per cent in 1951 to 39.29 per cent in 1991. Between 1981 and 1991, female literacy increased at a relatively faster pace of 9.6 per cent than male literacy which increased at 7.5 per cent. From 2001 to 2011, female literacy has increased from 54.2 per cent to 64.6 per cent.

The enrolment of girls in schools increased over thirtyfold from 0.5 million in 1950–1951 to 15.7 million in 1993–1994 at the middle school stage; and from 0.2 million to 8.1 million over the same period at the higher secondary stage.

115 **While enrolment has been growing:** During the period 1993–1994 more than one-third (39 per cent) of the number of girls enrolled at the primary stage dropped out before completing the primary level and more than half of them (about 57 per cent) dropped out before completing the middle stage; of the remainder (43 per cent) who reached the higher secondary stage, another 10 per cent dropped out before completing school. Thus only about 32 per cent of girls entering primary stage reached the end of schooling. In 2010-2011 the dropout rate of girls was 47.9 per cent at the secondary level.

116 *Unni Krishnan J. P. and Others:* AIR (1993) SC 2178.

WIDOWS' RIGHTS

Adapted from a talk given at the seminar on Widows' Rights, July 2000 (organized by Guild for Service).

130 **But it did not do away:** As a result of the 174th Law Commission Report, the law was amended in 2005 and daughters

Chapter Notes

also became coparceners with sons by The Hindu Succession (Amendment) Act, 2005.
131 **Raghubir Singh and Others:** AIR (1998) SC 2401.
131 **Vaddeboyina Tulasamma:** AIR (1977) SC 1944.
131 **Ram Kali:** (1997) 9 SCC 613.

PRISONERS' RIGHTS
Combined and adapted from the Sardar Patel Memorial Lecture, 2000 and the report of the Justice Leila Seth Commission of Inquiry (looking into the circumstances leading to the death of Janardhan Rajan Pillai), February 1997.
138 **The Supreme Court added:** *Sunil Batra vs Delhi Administration,* AIR (1980) SC 1579.
145 **Justice Krishna Iyer has said:** Ibid.
150 **Fortunately, in India:** In Central Jail, Tihar, Delhi, as of 28 February 2014, the number of undertrials lodged there was 10,419 (9,934 men and 485 women), about 75 per cent of the total population of 13,836.

JUDICIAL ADMINISTRATION
Adapted from a talk given at the Indo-British Legal Forum, 1989.
163 **In 1974 the Law Commission:** In 2011, in response to a question in the Rajya Sabha, Salman Khurshid, Minister of Law & Justice, informed the House that the government had proposed a number of measures to facilitate the expeditious disposal of cases in the courts. One of these measures was the setting up of a National Mission for Justice Delivery and Legal Reforms: the main objectives of this mission were to reduce delays and arrears in the system, to enhance accountability through structural changes, and to set performance standards and capacities.

To this end, the government accepted the recommendations of the 13th Finance Commission and provided a grant of ₹5,000 crore to the states for improving the justice delivery system over the five-year period 2010–2015. The states can, among other measures aimed at reducing pendency, set up morning-evening-shift/special magistrate courts, appoint court managers, establish Alternative Dispute Resolution (ADR) centres, provide training to mediators and conciliators, and organize more Lok Adalats.

170 *S. P. Gupta and Others:* AIR (1982) SC 149.

173 *Supreme Court Advocates-on-Record:* AIR (1994) SC 268.

173 **This position was clarified:** AIR (1999) SC 1.

184 **The process of:** This has been discussed in more detail in the essay 'Social Action Litigation'.

184 **The other reason:** A special leave petition is filed under Article 136 of the Constitution and seeks special leave to appeal against a judgment, decree, determination, sentence or order passed by any court or tribunal (not armed forces) in India. There is no right of appeal and it is dependent on the court's discretion to grant the special leave in exceptional cases of grave injustice.

187 **Many believe that:** *Additional District Magistrate Jabalpur vs Shivakant Shukla,* AIR (1976) SC 1207.

YOU'RE CRIMINAL IF GAY

First published in *The Times of India* (26 January 2014) as 'A Mother and a Judge Speaks Out on Section 377'.

References

RAPE: INSIDE THE JUSTICE VERMA COMMITTEE
Report of the Committee on Amendments to Criminal Law, 2013

GENDER SENSITIZATION OF THE JUDICIARY
'Dowry deaths: One woman dies every hour in India', *IBNLive*, 2 Sep 2013 <http://ibnlive.in.com/news/dowry-deaths-one-woman-dies-every-hour-in-india/419005-3.html> accessed 29 March 2014.

Abdulali, S. 1988. 'Rape in India: An Empirical Picture' in Rehana Ghadially (Ed.) *Women in Indian Society*.

Dine, J. and Watt, B. 'Sexual Harassment: Moving Away from Discrimination', *Modern Law Review*, 1995, Vol. 58, p. 343.

Dube, C. Making Equality Work, *The Indian Advocate*, Vol. VXXVII 1996–97, *Journal of the Bar Association of India*, p. 22.

Feingold, S. 'One rape every 20 minutes in country', *The Times of India*, 25 Aug 2013, <http://timesofindia.indiatimes.com/city/delhi/One-rape-every-20-minutes-in-country/articleshow/22040599.cms> accessed 29 March 2014.

Gender and Judges: A Judicial Point of View. 1996. Report by Sakshi.

Griffith, J. A. G. 1977. *The Politics of the Judiciary*.

Kapur, R. and Cossman, B. 1996. 'Constitutional Challenges and Contesting Discourses: Equality and Family', *Subversive Sites*.

Macmillan. 1948. *The Writing of Judgments*.

Mahajan, K. 1993. 'Indian Women. Victims of the Indian Constitution' in Kusum (Ed.) *Women: March Towards Dignity*.

Seth, L. 1993. 'On the Rights of the Child'. *IIC Quarterly,* Winter.

Seth, L. 1995. 'Gender Justice'. Paper read at the (Patna) Seminar on Gender Justice organized by the National Commission for Women.

Seth, L. 1997. 'Girl Child and Social Development', Durgabai Deshmukh Memorial Lecture.

Seth, L. 1996. 'Guaranteeing the Rights of Women and Children: International Protections', Paper read at the Seminar on Human Rights, an International Legal Perspective at Salzburg, Austria.

Seth, L. 1995. 'Social Action Litigation in India' in Liebenberg, S (Ed.) *The Constitution of South Africa from a Gender Perspective.*

Sinha, B. '"Indian judiciary needs more women", says CJI designate', *Hindustan Times,* 3 Jul 2013 <http://www.hindustantimes.com/india-news/newdelhi/indian-judiciary-needs-more-women-says-cji-designate/article1-1086111.aspx> accessed 28 March 2014.

SOCIAL ACTION LITIGATION

Agrawal, S. K. 1985. *Public Interest Litigation in India.*

Basu, D. D. 1994. *Shorter Constitution of India.*

Chopra, S. 1985. 'Public Interest Litigation: An Appraisal', working paper delivered at the 9th Lawasia Conference, New Delhi.

Choudhary, S. R. 1985. 'Status of *Locus Standi* in Different Legal Systems', working paper delivered at the 9th Lawasia Conference, New Delhi.

Mcmullin, D. W. 1985. 'Public Interest Litigation', working paper delivered at the 9th Lawasia Conference, New Delhi.

Misra, P. C. 1985. 'Public Interest Litigation: A Brief Conspectus', working paper delivered at the 9th Lawasia Conference, New Delhi.

Mridul, M. 1986. 'Public Interest Litigation: A Profile', *Bharat Law Times.*

Ramakrishna, J. (Ed). 1993. *Women in India: Reflecting on our History and Shaping our Future* (Netherlands, Humanistic Institute for Co-operation with Developing Countries, 1993); report of HIVOS (Humanist Institute for Cooperation) and Centre for Women's Development Studies (New Delhi) consultation, Bangalore.

Reddy, O. C. 1990. *From a Man's World to a Human World.*

Seth, L. 1985. 'How Far are the Penal Laws Effective in Protecting Women?', working paper delivered at the 9th Lawasia Conference, New Delhi.

Tripathi, S. M. 1993. *The Human Face of the Supreme Court of India.*

Venkataramiah, E. S. 1986. *Women and the Law.*

WOMEN'S RIGHTS

'Facts & Figures on Women, Poverty & Economics' UN Women, (undated), <http://www.unifem.org/gender_issues/women_poverty_economics/facts_figures.html> accessed 4 April 2014.

'Women, Poverty and Economics, UN Women, (undated), <http://www.unifem.org/gender_issues/women_poverty_economics/> accessed 30 April 2014.

Census of India, 2001, Series 1 – India, Registrar General and Census Commissioner, India.

Census of India, 2011, Provisional Population Totals, Series 1 – India, Registrar General and Census Commissioner, India.

Cook, R. J. (Ed.) 1994. 'Women's International Human Rights Law: The Way Forward', *Human Rights of Women: National and International Perspectives.*

Cook, R. J. (Ed.) 1994. 'State Accountability under the Convention on the Elimination of All Forms of Discrimination against Women' *Human Rights of Women: National and International Perspectives.*

Coomaraswamy, R. 1994. 'To Bellow Like a Cow: Women, Ethnicity, and the Discourse of Rights' in Cook, R. J. (Ed.) *Human Rights of Women: National and International Perspectives.*

Higgins, R. 1994. 'World Conference on Human Rights', *Journal of United Lawyers' Association.*

Hossain, S. 1994. 'Equality in the Home: Women's Rights and Personal Laws in South Asia' in Cook, R. J. (Ed.) *Human Rights of Women: National and International Perspectives.*

Human Development Report 2001, United Nations Development Programme.

Singh, K. 1994. 'Obstacles to Women's Rights in India' in Cook, R. J. (Ed.) *Human Rights of Women: National and International Perspectives*.
Vij, S. 'A Mighty Heart', *Tehelka*, 13 Oct 2007.

A UNIFORM CIVIL CODE TOWARDS GENDER JUSTICE

'Law to Give Hindu Women Equal Rights', *The Times of India*, 4 Dec 2004.
'The Long Road to Gender Equality', *The Hindu*, 7 Dec 2004.
Aiyar, M. S. 2006. *Confessions of a Secular Fundamentalist*.
Ali, M. 'SC ruling does not interfere with Muslim personal law', *The Hindu*, 22 Feb 2014.
Chatterjee, S. 'Constitution, Parliament and the People', *The Hindu*, 8 Dec 2004.
Dhagamwar, V. 1996. *Reading on Uniform Civil Code and Gender and Child Just Laws*.
Seth, L. 2003. *On Balance*.

CHILDREN'S RIGHTS

'Education', UNICEF, (undated) <http://www.unicef.org/india/children_2359.htm> accessed 28 March 2014.
'India's literacy rate rises to 73 per cent as population growth dips', *Mail Online India*, 1 May 2013 <http://www.dailymail.co.uk/indiahome/indianews/article-2317341/Indias-literacy-rate-rises-73-cent-population-growth-dips.html> accessed 28 March 2014.
'The Indian Clusters: An Overview of the Carpet Industry', 2004. D'Essence Consulting, <http://www.dessenceconsulting.com/pdf/Carpet.pdf> accessed 28 March 2014.
Bahree, M. 'Your Beautiful Indian Rug Was Probably Made By Child Labor', *Forbes*, 2 May 2014 <http://www.forbes.com/sites/meghabahree/2014/02/05/your-beautiful-indian-rug-was-probably-made-by-child-labor> accessed 28 March 2014.
Carpet Industry in India, India Brand Equity Foundation, (undated), <http://www.ibef.org/exports/carpet-industry-in-india.aspx> accessed 28 March 2014.

References

Census of India, 2001, Series 1 – India, Registrar General and Census Commissioner, India.

Census of India, 2011, Provisional Population Totals, Series 1 – India, Registrar General and Census Commissioner, India.

Chamberlain, G. 'Rescuers fear India will drop new law banning child labour', *The Observer*, 23 Feb 2013 <http://www.theguardian.com/law/2013/feb/23/india-law-child-labour> accessed 28 March 2014.

Human Development Report 2001, United Nations Development Programme, Oxford University Press, New York.

Seth, L. 1993. 'The Rights of the Child' *IIC Quarterly*, Winter.

'The State of the World's Children' 2001, UNICEF – United Nations Children's Fund.

Weiner, M. 1991. *The Child and the State in India*.

THE GIRL CHILD

'Average Age at Marriage – India', MedIndia (undated) <http://www.medindia.net/health_statistics/general/marriageage.asp> accessed 1 Apr 2014.

'Impressive growth in enrolment of girls in schools: Survey', *The Indian Express*, 22 Jan 2013 < http://archive.indianexpress.com/news/impressive-growth-in-enrolment-of-girls-in-schools-survey/1062623/> accessed 1 Apr 2014.

'The Girl Child', *Focus on Women*, 1995. UN Department of Public Information, New York.

A Module for Awareness on Survival, Protection and Development of the Girl Child, Central Social Welfare Board, New Delhi.

Amirtham, N. and Kundupuzhakkal, S. 2013. 'Gender Issues and Dropout Rates in India: Major Barrier in Providing Education for All', *Confab Journals* Vol. 2, No. 4.

Bhalla, S. S. and Kaur, R. 'The Girl Child's Future', *Indian Express*, 5 Nov 2012.

Deshmukh, D. 1980. *Chintaman and I*.

Deshmukh, D. 1979. *The Stone that Speaketh*.

Dhagamwar, V. 1996. *Reading on Uniform Civil Code and Gender and Child Just Laws*.

Dhar, A. 'Children Having Children and Dying', *The Hindu*, 29 Jun 2012.

Dhawan, H. 'India has 40% of world's child brides, survey finds', *The Times of India*, 9 Sep 2013, <http://articles.timesofindia.indiatimes.com/2013-09-09/india/41903186_1_child-brides-gaya-18-years> accessed 1 Apr 2014.

Education Commission Report, 1964–67.

Gupta, S. D., Mukherjee, S., Singh, S., Pande, R. and Basu, S. 2008. *Knot Ready, Lessons from India on Delaying Marriage for Girls*, ICRW (International Centre for Research on Women).

Human Development Report, 1997. UNDP.

India Country Report for the Fourth World Conference on Women, Beijing, 1995.

India: The Road to Human Development. 1997. UNDP.

Jain, D. 1996. *Minds, Bodies and Exemplars*.

Jejeebhoy, S. J. 1997. 'Addressing Women's Reproductive Health Needs', *Economic and Political Weekly* Volume XXXII, Nos. 9 and 10, March 1–8, 1997.

Mehta, P. B. 'By Her Yardstick', *The Indian Express*, 22 Jun 2012.

Mukherji, A. 'Village Vows to Let Girls Live', *The Times of India*, 17 Jul 2012.

Naqvi, F., Kumar, A. K. S. 'India and the Sex Selection Conundrum', *The Hindu*, 24 Jan 2012.

National Plan of Action. 1992. Government of India, Department of Women and Child Development, Ministry of Human Resource Development.

Perappadan, B. S. 'Too Young to Tie the Knot', *The Hindu*, 3 Jul 2012.

Rajalakshmi, T. K. 'Off Target', *Frontline*, 14–27 Jan 2012.

Ramaseshan, G. 'Law and the Age of Innocence', *The Hindu*, 19 Jun 2012.

Report on Prevention of Child Marriages in the State of Karnataka by the Core Committee. 2011. Headed by Justice Shivraj V. Patil,

UNICEF and Department of Women and Child Development.
Anandalakshmy. S. (Ed.) 1994. 'The Girl Child and the Family', An Action Research Study.
Sadik, N. 1997. *The State of World Population*
Seth, L. 1995. 'Gender Justice'. Paper read at the (Patna) Seminar on Gender Justice organized by the National Commission for Women.
Seth, L. 1995. 'The Rights of the Child', *IIC Quarterly,* Winter.
Seth, L. 1996. 'Guaranteeing the Rights of Women and Children International Protections'. Paper read at the Seminar on Human Rights, an International Perspective at Salzburg, Austria.
Paniker, R. and Desai, K. 1992. *Street Girls of Delhi: Case Studies,* Child Labour Cell, VV Giri National Labour Institute.
Baig, T.A. 1996. *India's Women Power.*
United Nations Report on the Fourth World Conference on Women, 1995. Beijing, China.
Yi, Z., et al., 1993. 'Causes and Implications of the Recent Increase in the Reported Sex Ratio at Birth in China', *Population and Development Review,* 19: 2.
Youth in India: Situation and Trends, 2006–07.

WIDOWS' RIGHTS

Chakravarti, U. 1998. *Rewriting History: The Life and Times of Pandita Ramabai.*
Chen, M.A., (Ed.) 1998. *Widows in India: Social Neglect and Public Action.*
Mayne, J. D. *Hindu Law and Usage,* Fourteenth Edition.
Mulla, D. F. 1998. *Principles of Hindu Law.*
'Property Rights of Women: Proposed Reforms under the Hindu Law'. 2000. *174th Report of the Law Commission of India.*
Ray, B. and Basu, A. (Ed.) 1999. *From Independence Towards Freedom: Indian Women Since 1947.*
'Repeal of the Hindu Widows Remarriage Act, 1856'. 1979. *81st Report of the Law Commission of India.*

PRISONERS' RIGHTS

'All countries compared for Crime', The Eighth United Nations Survey on Crime Trends and the Operations of Criminal Justice Systems (2002) (United Nations Office on Drugs and Crime, Centre for International Crime Prevention).

'Code of Criminal Procedure'. 1996. *154th Report of the Law Commission of India.*

'Congestion of Undertrial Prisoners in Jails'. 1979. *78th Report of the Law Commission of India.*

All India Committee on Jail Reforms, 1980–1983 (Mulla Committee).

Annual Report 1997–1998, National Human Rights Commission.

Justice Leila Seth Commission of Inquiry (looking into the circumstances leading to the death of Janardhan Rajan Pillai), Home Department, Government of the National Capital Territory of Delhi, 1997.

Making Standards Work: An International Handbook on Good Prison Practice Penal Reform International, 1995, The Hague.

National Offender Management Service Annual Report and Accounts 2010-11. United Kingdom.

Pathak, R. S. 1998. Foreword in Venkataramiah (Ed.) *Human Rights in the Changing World*

Prison Statistics India, 2012.

Prisoner Profile <http://www.delhi.gov.in/wps/wcm/connect/lib_centraljail/Central+Jail/Home/Prisoner+Profile> accessed 15 April 2014.

Lillich, R. B. 2006. *International Human Rights: Problems of Law, Policy and Practice.*

Sharma, K. 'Deaths double inside Tihar, poor health care to blame?', *The Hindu*, 21 Feb 2014.

Stern, V. 1998. *A Sin against the Future: Imprisonment in the World.*

Travis, A. 'Brixton prison: "you can get drugs but not clean underwear"', *The Guardian*, 17 Dec 2013 <http://www.theguardian.com/society/2013/dec/17/brixton-prison-drugs-underwear-inspection-report-cramped> accessed 15 April 2014.

References

Women Prisoners in Indian Jails, National Commission for Women.

Workshop on Prisons and Human Rights, April 25–26, 1998, Bhopal, jointly organized by Madhya Pradesh Human Rights Commission and the Commonwealth Human Rights Initiative.

World Prison Populations, BBC (Source: International Centre for Prison Studies) <http://news.bbc.co.uk/2/shared/spl/hi/uk/06/prisons/html/nn2page1.stm> accessed 15 April 2014.

JUDICIAL ADMINISTRATION

'Delay and arrears in High Courts and other Appellate Courts'. 1979. *79th Report of Law Commission of India*.

'Delay and arrears in trial courts'. 1978. *77th Report of Law Commission of India*.

'Litigation by and against the Government: Some recommendations for reform'. 1984. *100th Report of Law Commission of India*.

'Manpower Planning in Judiciary: A Blueprint'. 1987. *120th Report of Law Commission of India*.

'Moily: adopt campaign mode for speedy justice', *The Hindu,* 12 May 2011 http://www.thehindu.com/news/national/moily-adopt-campaign-mode-for-speedy-justice/article2008922.ece> accessed 25 April 2014.

'Oral and written arguments in the Higher Courts'. 1984. *99th Report of Law Commission of India*.

'Reform of Judicial Administration'. 1958. *14th Report of Law Commission of India*.

'Structure and Jurisdiction of the Higher Judiciary'. 1974. *58th Report of Law Commission of India*.

Tarkunde, V. M. 'Challenges to the Judiciary and the Legal Profession' (Seth Chhotelal Memorial Lecture).

Khanna, H. R. 1985. 'Judiciary in India and Judicial Process', Tagore Law Lectures.

Nehru, B. K. 1985. 'The Administration of Justice', Lecture under the auspices of Documentation Centre for Corporate and Business Policy Research.

Note of the Karnataka High Court on Jurisdictional Reforms of the Supreme Court and High Courts with reference to the Resolution of the Chief Justices' Conference, 1988.

Press Information Bureau, Govt. of India, M/o Law & Justice, cases pending in the High Court and Supreme Court http://pib.nic.in/newsite/erelease.aspx?relid=73624> accessed 30 April 2014.

Supreme Court of India, Monthly Pending Cases, <http://supremecourtofindia.nic.in/pendingstat.htm> accessed 25 April 2014.

The Position of the Judiciary under the Constitution of India by H. M. Seervai (Sir Chimanlal Setalvad Lectures).

The Summary of Recommendations of the Committee of Three Chief Justices set up by the Government of India pursuant to a Resolution of the Chief Justices' Conference, 1983, to study the problem of arrears in High Courts and suggest reforms.